WARBIRD**TECH**
S E R I E S

VOLUME 16

LOCKHEED
U-2 DRAGON LADY

BY DENNIS R. JENKINS

specialtypress
PUBLISHERS AND WHOLESALERS

Specialty Press
39966 Grand Avenue
North Branch, MN 55056
Phone: 651-277-1400 or 800-895-4585
Fax: 651-277-1203
www.specialtypress.com

© 1998 Dennis R. Jenkins

All rights reserved. No part of this publication may be reproduced or utilized in any form or by any means, electronic or mechanical, including photocopying, recording, or by any information storage and retrieval system, without prior permission from the Publisher. All text, photographs, and artwork are the property of the Author unless otherwise noted or credited.

The information in this work is true and complete to the best of our knowledge. However, all information is presented without any guarantee on the part of the Author or Publisher, who also disclaim any liability incurred in connection with the use of the information and any implied warranties of merchantability or fitness for a particular purpose. Readers are responsible for taking suitable and appropriate safety measures when performing any of the operations or activities described in this work.

All trademarks, trade names, model names and numbers, and other product designations referred to herein are the property of their respective owners and are used solely for identification purposes. This work is a publication of CarTech, Inc., and has not been licensed, approved, sponsored, or endorsed by any other person or entity. The publisher is not associated with any product, service, or vendor mentioned in this book, and does not endorse the products or services of any vendor mentioned in this book.

Design by Greg Compton

ISBN 978-1-158007-200-7
Item No. SP009P

Printed in U.S.A.

Distributed in the UK and Europe by

Crécy Publishing Ltd
1a Ringway Trading Estate
Shadowmoss Road
Manchester M22 5LH England
Tel: 44 161 499 0024
Fax : 44 161 499 0298
www.crecy.co.uk
enquiries@crecy.co.uk

TABLE OF CONTENTS

THE DOUGLAS A-1 SKYRAIDER

PREFACE **4**
A WORD FROM THE AUTHOR

CHAPTER 1: THE ARTICLE **5**
AQUATONE, IDEALIST AND ANGEL

CHAPTER 2: SMALL WING DRAGON LADIES **12**
THE U-2A THROUGH U-2H

CHAPTER 3: EARLY U-2 OPERATIONS **30**
DRAGONS OVER RUSSIA AND CHINA

CHAPTER 4: BIG WING DRAGON LADIES **40**
THE U-2R

CHAPTER 5: IMAGES FROM LARGE DRAGONS **50**
THE U-2R BECOMES OPERATIONAL

CHAPTER 6: TACTICAL SPYPLANES **54**
BACK IN PRODUCTION, AGAIN

SPECIAL SECTION: THE LADY SHOWS HER COLORS **65**
NOT ALWAYS BLACK OR WHITE

CHAPTER 7: PHOTOGRAPHING SADAM **74**
BATTLEFIELD RECONNAISSANCE

CHAPTER 8: TAMING THE DRAGON **88**
WHITE AND BLUE U-2S

APPENDIX: CODE NAMES **97**
DECIPHERING THE ALPHABET SOUP

SIGNIFICANT DATES **100**
KEY DATES IN THE HISTORY OF THE U-2 DRAGON LADY

PREFACE

A WORD FROM THE AUTHOR

The U-2 made the Lockheed Skunk Works. Although Lockheed's Clarence L. "Kelly" Johnson was already an established aircraft designer, and what is now known as Skunk Works had conceived and built the XP-80 Shooting Star and XF-104 Starfighter prototypes, it was the CIA's decision to let Lockheed design and build the U-2 that cemented Skunk Works' reputation.

Part of this was due to how the contract was won. Kelly Johnson, his initial unsolicited proposal rejected by the Air Force, went through a back door to the Central Intelligence Agency and landed a contract for 20 aircraft – with the condition the first one fly less than a year later. Johnson made that milestone, and returned $8 million from the original $54 million contract; one of the rare instances of cost underruns in modern aerospace history.

The aircraft itself has helped sustain both its own and Skunk Works' legend. It is one of the few aircraft types ordered back into production, in this case twice. The second production run, admittedly of a much different variant, occurred ten years after the original. The third run was 12 years after the second, although this time the aircraft were for all intents identical to the second batch.

Much of the U-2's history and current operations remains classified. But the aircraft has been in constant service for over 40 years, and numerous details have made their way into the public domain. The aircraft continues to provide remarkable service even though its demise was predicted 30 years ago when spy satellites became the intelligence community's technology of choice. Interestingly, the Dragon Lady has long outlived its heir apparent, the Mach 3+ A-12 Blackbird, another Kelly Johnson design. There are currently no plans to phase the U-2 out of service, and efforts to replace it with Unmanned Aerial Vehicles (UAV) are running into considerable development delays.

It's hard to tell the story of the U-2 without using many codenames and acronyms. In some ways this makes reading more difficult, but it also makes it possible to believe you are in a James Bond novel, something the U-2 probably inspired in more ways than one.

It is impossible to provide a detailed accounting of all the Dragon Lady's 45 years in a short monograph. Luckily, there have been several excellent books on the U-2. Although beginning to age slightly, Chris Pocock's *Dragon Lady: The History of the U-2 Spyplane* remains the most far-ranging work on the subject. Fortunately, Chris is in the process of updating this excellent work, which is a "must read" for anybody interested in the U-2. Jay Miller's *Skunk Works: The Official History* has extensive coverage of the U-2. Not surprisingly, Aerofax's *Minigraph #28* on the U-2R/TR-1 is also a detailed work, having been co-written by Chris and Jay. Chris also wrote an excellent article for the Spring 1997 volume (#28) of the *World Air Power Journal*. Any of these makes for a fascinating insight into the still classified world of the Dragon Lady.

This book would not have been possible without a great deal of assistance. Mick Roth, as always, provided terrific assistance in locating data and images. Chris Pocock and Jay Miller contributed data without compromising the worth of their great works. Coy F. Cross II, the 9th Reconnaissance Wing Historian, provided an excellent insight into operations during the Gulf War. Denny Lombard at the Skunk Works and Tony Landis gave me access to their extensive collections of photographs, many of which appear herein. And many thanks to my mother, Mrs. Mary E. Jenkins, who always inspired me to write, and who continues to provide critical encouragement.

On 7 February 1998, famed Lockheed test pilot Tony LeVier passed away. Among other feats, he was the first pilot to tame the Dragon Lady. He will be sorely missed by the aviation community.

One of the first in-flight photographs of the U-2 released to the public. (Lockheed Martin)

THE ARTICLE

AQUATONE, IDEALIST AND ANGEL

During World War II, most aerial reconnaissance was conducted by modified combat types – P-38s, P-51s, and B-29s equipped with cameras. Towards the end of the war, recognizing the need for more dedicated machines, the Army Air Corps initiated the development of the Hughes XF-11 and Republic XF-12 Rainbow. Both aircraft were powered by Pratt & Whitney R-4360-31 radial piston engines, although they were very different approaches to the concept. Neither of these aircraft entered production, but they demonstrated the substantial increase in capabilities available in designs tailored for the mission. The decrease in defense spending following the end of the war, however, meant that combat types would continue to be used for reconnaissance. The Air Force pressed modified B-36, B-45, and B-50 bombers, as well as a variety of fighters, into service as reconnaissance aircraft.

By 1952 thoughts again turned to a dedicated high-altitude platform, and in March 1953 a formal specification was completed. After being reviewed and approved by the Pentagon, this specification was released to three small aircraft manufacturers. All three companies, Bell, Fairchild, and Martin, received six-month $200,000 study contracts on 1 July 1953. The new project was identified as MX-2147 and used the codename BALD EAGLE. Only Bell and Fairchild were asked to design new aircraft to meet the specification. Martin was

tasked with designing a modification to their B-57 Canberra, which had originally been designed in the UK by the English Electric Company.

Air Force and Pratt & Whitney engineers had already conducted preliminary research into converting the J57 axial-flow turbojet into a high altitude engine. Proposed modifications to the J57 were expected to permit a sustained high altitude operating thrust of approximately 7% of the available sea-level thrust. Though far from impressive, even by 1954 standards, it was adequate in the rarefied atmosphere to power any of the aircraft being contemplated. Other powerplants, notably the General

Electric J73 and Wright J67, were considered by the contractors during the course of the study, but there was never any serious doubt the J57 would be selected.

In January 1954 the three companies submitted their proposals to the Air Force, all choosing the J57 engine. As requested, Martin presented their Model 294, which was little more than a B-57 fuselage mated to a larger wing containing two J57 engines. Although it could not reach the requested 70,000 feet, it could be produced quickly and inexpensively. The Bell Model 67 was a fragile-looking aircraft with two J57 engines mounted on a high aspect ratio wing that

The first Article at Groom Lake was devoid of any markings except a national insignia and a small "001" on the vertical stabilizer. The "001" on the tail would disappear shortly. Officially this was Article 341, and the aircraft was lost before an Air Force serial number could be assigned. The first Article did not have the "sugar scoop" under the engine exhaust that was added to provide a small margin of shielding against the Soviets detecting the engine heat. (Lockheed Martin Skunk Works via Denny Lombard)

The U-2A was a very simple aircraft, and could be manufactured and maintained with a minimum set of specialized equipment. Reportedly this is the first Article while it was being reassembled at Groom lake. (Lockheed Martin)

spanned 115 feet. Fairchild offered the single-engine M-195 with a dorsal air intake and boom-mounted tail surfaces. The aircraft weighed an amazing 11,000 pounds empty, less than half that of the Bell design.

By the middle of 1954 it had been decided the Martin RB-57D would be procured as an interim platform pending the development of the Bell Model 67. Fairchild's proposal was never in serious contention due to its unconventional configuration. The competition was disrupted, however, on 18 May 1954 when an unsolicited proposal was received from Lockheed's famed Kelly Johnson.

During December 1953, for reasons that are not completely clear, Johnson had begun exploring the feasibility of modifying the new XF-104 interceptor into a high altitude reconnaissance platform. By March 1954 this had progressed to the point that Johnson published Lockheed Report #9732 describing a proposed CL-282 high-altitude air-

craft. This report was sent to the Air Force just as the BALD EAGLE competition was being concluded.

The design had the basic fuselage of the XF-104A with a new 500 square-foot wing that used an aspect ratio of 10:1 over its 70.66 foot span. The fuselage had been shortened 62 inches to 44 feet by removing a straight section ahead of the air intakes, and the F-104's tee-tail was retained. An unusual design feature was the omission of landing gear from the aircraft. A special ground cart was provided for taxi and take-off, and landing was accomplished on a reinforced belly, much like civilian sailplanes.

The CL-282 was to be capable of achieving 73,000 feet with an operating radius of 1,600 miles. The aircraft had a normal gross takeoff weight of 13,768 pounds, including 4,966 pounds of fuel and a non-jettisonable 600 pound payload. An overload weight of 14,815 pounds enabled a radius of 1,980 miles by carrying 160 gallons more fuel in underwing drop tanks. This perfor-

mance was achieved using a single General Electric J73-GE-3 engine. The single seat cockpit was unpressurized and not equipped with an ejection seat while the payload was carried in an unpressurized 15 cubic foot compartment immediately behind the cockpit.

The Air Force conducted a thorough, if somewhat hurried, review and decided the major drawbacks were the use of the J73 powerplant, the unpressurized cockpit, and limited range compared to the Bell proposal. The Air Force did not believe (correctly, as it turned out) that the J73 would mature sufficiently to be used in the timeframe required. Also, since very little study had been conducted on the high altitude performance of the J73 there were concerns over its performance outside its normal design envelope. On 7 June 1954, Kelly Johnson was informed by letter that his proposal had been rejected.

After the Air Force declined to select Lockheed's proposal, Johnson decided to pursue funding through other channels. This essentially meant the Central Intelligence Agency (CIA) which had discovered that the military services could be not be depended upon to provide detailed reconnaissance whenever and wherever the CIA wanted it. Conflicting priorities within the military, and inter-agency rivalry, where the primary causes. And since the Soviet Union was embarking on a crash program to develop

GENERAL CONFIGURATION - MODEL U-2C

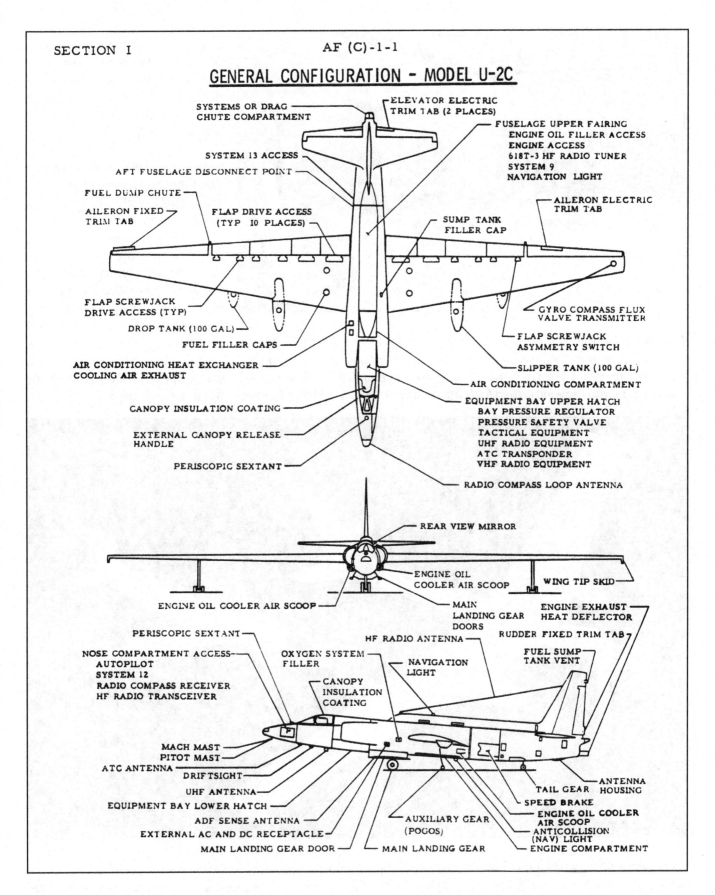

SYSTEMS OR DRAG CHUTE COMPARTMENT

ELEVATOR ELECTRIC TRIM TAB (2 PLACES)

FUSELAGE UPPER FAIRING
ENGINE OIL FILLER ACCESS
ENGINE ACCESS
618T-3 HF RADIO TUNER
SYSTEM 9
NAVIGATION LIGHT

SYSTEM 13 ACCESS

AFT FUSELAGE DISCONNECT POINT

FUEL DUMP CHUTE

AILERON FIXED TRIM TAB

FLAP DRIVE ACCESS (TYP 10 PLACES)

AILERON ELECTRIC TRIM TAB

SUMP TANK FILLER CAP

FLAP SCREWJACK DRIVE ACCESS (TYP)

DROP TANK (100 GAL)

FUEL FILLER CAPS

GYRO COMPASS FLUX VALVE TRANSMITTER

FLAP SCREWJACK ASYMMETRY SWITCH

AIR CONDITIONING HEAT EXCHANGER COOLING AIR EXHAUST

SLIPPER TANK (100 GAL)

AIR CONDITIONING COMPARTMENT

CANOPY INSULATION COATING

EQUIPMENT BAY UPPER HATCH
BAY PRESSURE REGULATOR
PRESSURE SAFETY VALVE
TACTICAL EQUIPMENT
UHF RADIO EQUIPMENT
ATC TRANSPONDER
VHF RADIO EQUIPMENT

EXTERNAL CANOPY RELEASE HANDLE

PERISCOPIC SEXTANT

RADIO COMPASS LOOP ANTENNA

REAR VIEW MIRROR

ENGINE OIL COOLER AIR SCOOP

WING TIP SKID

ENGINE OIL COOLER AIR SCOOP

MAIN LANDING GEAR DOORS

ENGINE EXHAUST HEAT DEFLECTOR

HF RADIO ANTENNA

RUDDER FIXED TRIM TAB

PERISCOPIC SEXTANT

OXYGEN SYSTEM FILLER

NAVIGATION LIGHT

FUEL SUMP TANK VENT

NOSE COMPARTMENT ACCESS
AUTOPILOT
SYSTEM 12
RADIO COMPASS RECEIVER
HF RADIO TRANSCEIVER

CANOPY INSULATION COATING

MACH MAST
PITOT MAST

ATC ANTENNA

DRIFTSIGHT

UHF ANTENNA

EQUIPMENT BAY LOWER HATCH

ADF SENSE ANTENNA

EXTERNAL AC AND DC RECEPTACLE

MAIN LANDING GEAR DOOR

AUXILIARY GEAR (POGOS)

MAIN LANDING GEAR

ANTENNA HOUSING

TAIL GEAR

SPEED BRAKE

ENGINE OIL COOLER AIR SCOOP

ANTICOLLISION (NAV) LIGHT

ENGINE COMPARTMENT

The U-2C general configuration drawing from a 1968 edition of the U-2C/F flight manual shows few surprises, but does list the location of most of the antennas carried on the aircraft. (U.S. Air Force)

Manufacturing the U-2's wing proved to be one of the critical items in getting the first Article ready for its maiden flight. The unconventional structure required to meet the weight restrictions demanded a great deal of care during construction, and the wing proved fairly fragile in operation. (Lockheed Martin)

and field long-range missiles equipped with nuclear warheads, the CIA considered on-demand intelligence critical. The obvious answer was to create a private air arm.

Concurrently with contacting the CIA, Johnson embarked on modifying the Lockheed design to accommodate the J57 engine and a more conventional landing gear. This time the F-104 fuselage was extensively modified with the exception of the cockpit area which was retained relatively intact. Pressurization was added for the cockpit and payload bay, and the tee-tail configuration was traded for a more conventional arrangement.

Bell's Model 67 (later designated X-16) used two J57 engines mounted at mid-span on each wing. The pods on the wing tips housed retractable pogo landing gear, although by the time the mock-up review was completed these were mounted just outboard of the engine nacelles. The X-16 was cancelled based mainly on the success of the U-2A. Noteworthy is the X-16's size compared to the F-86. (U.S. Air Force)

Deceptions within the government. This was the first public showing of the U-2A, conducted at the NASA Flight Research Center in 1960. The NASA markings are decidedly fictitious, having been applied only an hour or so before the press arrived after the aircraft was flown from North Base to the NASA facility. The "55741" serial number is also quite fictitious. (NASA/DFRC via the Tony Landis Collection)

On 19 November 1954 Johnson discussed the modified design with the intelligence community. The proposal generated a great deal of interest, assuming Lockheed could deliver the aircraft quickly. Two days later Johnson met with senior Lockheed management to convince them to allow the Skunk Works to design and manufacture the aircraft. This was a departure from the norm, where Skunk Works designed aircraft, and perhaps built the first prototype, but turned production over to other divisions within Lockheed. In this case Johnson deemed it necessary to keep the project totally in-house to preserve its secrecy and meet the promised schedule. His bosses agreed, and a dynasty was born.

The next ten days were spent refining the design, increasing its payload capacity slightly, and making sure the new engine would fit correctly. Johnson promised the first aircraft would fly by September 1955, less than a year in the future. At the end of November the CIA formally approved the project under the codename AQUATONE, and Johnson was notified. A $54 million contract for 20 production aircraft was signed on 9 December 1954, although Johnson would later return almost $8 million of this due to cost underruns! Interestingly, most of the money reportedly changed hands through Johnson's private bank accounts in an effort to disguise what was happening,

The U-2s normally took pictures of the ground. However, on many occasions the ground took pictures of U-2s. Here one of the Edwards' U-2s has been painted with a series of photo reference markings for calibrating a ground-based camera. (U.S. Air Force via the Tony Landis Collection)

One of the Edwards U-2s flies over the North American XB-70A Valkyrie experimental bomber. (U.S. Air Forces via the Tony Landis Collection)

tract was signed, the AQUATONE design was frozen. Ten days later construction of production tooling was begun. Around this time the aircraft became known within Skunk Works as "Kelly's Angel" or simply as ANGEL. The CIA assigned a second codename to the project, IDEALIST, but this was seldom used by anybody. The individual aircraft would be known as "articles."

The X-16 (as the Model 67 had been officially designated) progressed at Bell while AQUATONE gathered momentum at Skunk Works. Though a relatively small contract, the X-16 was important to Bell's economic future at a time when the company had few other major projects on its ledger. In October 1955, some two months after AQUATONE's first flight, the X-16 was cancelled as redundant. The loss of the contract proved to be a serious economic blow to Bell, and one from which the company would never truly recover.

although exactly how Johnson explained this sudden large increase in apparent salary to the IRS remains a mystery.

By the end of 1954, Johnson and his team of 25 engineers and 81 shop personnel began working 100 hour weeks in order to meet the schedule. While Johnson did eventually get additional personnel, he never had more than 80 engineers working on the U-2 project.

The design was technologically demanding since minimum weight and drag were essential. On 10 December, one day after the con-

Wind tunnel testing of ANGEL was completed on 15 March 1955 with no major surprises. By May 1955 the first fuselage was in the production jig, but the wing was presenting challenges to the shop crew. Johnson's unique lightweight design was proving more difficult than expected to manufacture. The problems were overcome by the beginning of July and the first aircraft was completed on 15 July. The next day the aircraft was partially disassembled for loading aboard a C-124 transport bound for the flight test location at Groom Lake.

A U-2A taxies in front of its genetic mother, an F-104. Although based loosely on the same idea, the aircraft could not have been further apart in performance. The F-104 could break Mach 2, but could only stay airborne for a short time. The U-2 was slow, but stayed airborne for nine hours at a stretch. (Lockheed Martin)

GENERAL CONFIGURATION - MODEL U-2F

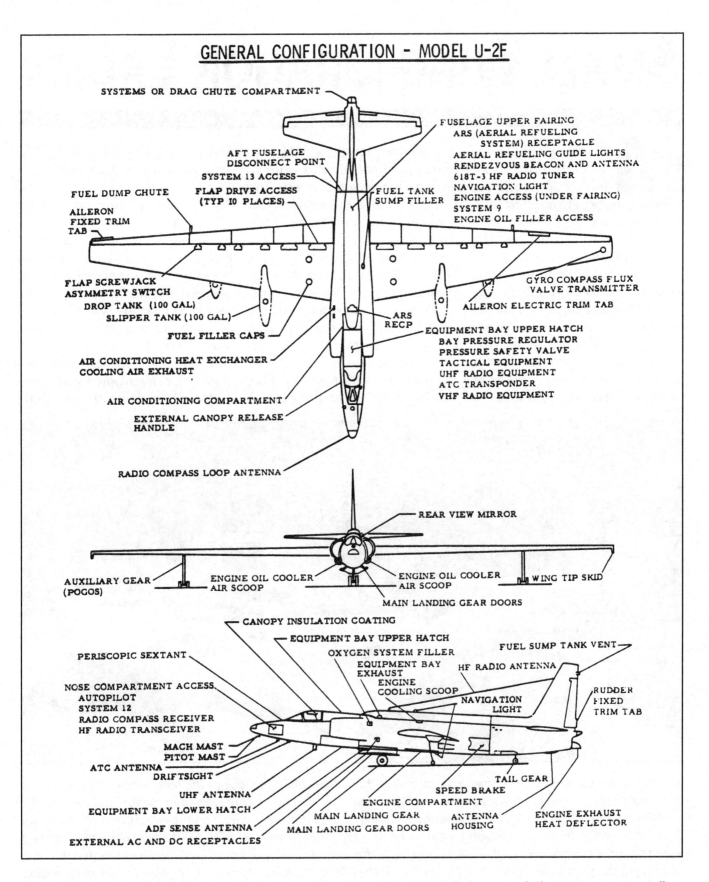

The U-2F general configuration drawing from a 1968 edition of the U-2C/F flight manual. The U-2F was essentially a U-2C fitted for aerial refueling, although a few systems were rearranged in order to accommodate the refueling equipment. The external fuel tanks could not be refueled in flight. (U.S. Air Force)

SMALL WING DRAGON LADIES

THE U-2A THROUGH U-2H

Mid-morning on 24 July 1955, the first U-2A (Article 341) arrived at Groom Lake, better known to Lockheed personnel at the time as the "Test Location," or simply "The Ranch." The subject of much speculation and many rumors over the years, Groom Lake is located inside a restricted area (Area 51) near the nuclear test site run by the Department of Energy (originally, the Atomic Energy Commission). It is located approximately 100 miles northwest of Las Vegas, Nevada.

It took Lockheed two days to reassemble the aircraft prior to engine run-ups and taxi tests. This first U-2 differed in several details from ones that would follow. A canvas sunshade was mounted on support cords over the pilot – later aircraft would have one painted on the inside of the canopy. The wingtip skid-plates extended rearward to the trailing edge of the wing instead of terminating at the aileron hinge. Also, the aircraft was not equipped with the drag chute housing above the engine exhaust,

and was missing the pilot's drift-sight and associated optical ports.

The U-2 was an unusual aircraft. Although the design had started out as a modification of the basic F-104 fuselage, the final aircraft bore little but a superficial resemblance to the Starfighter. The 49.66-foot long fuselage was a conventional monocoque structure using aluminum alloys. The 80.10-foot wings were of three spar construction, but conventional ribs were replaced by an unusual lattice work

U-2A maintenance was often carried out under less than ideal conditions due to the remote operating locations dictated by security and proximity to the overflight area. Two J57 engines are located in the foreground, and the small work stands used to support the wingtips during maintenance are visible on the closest aircraft. Although difficult to notice, the closest aircraft is configured as a DIRTY BIRD with an ECHOSORB radar absorbing coating over the entire exterior. This coating was not terribly effective, and also prevented heat transfer from the airframe, causing at least one in-flight accident. Noteworthy is the NACA insignia on the vertical stabilizer in the background, a ruse often employed by the early U-2 operations. Note the complete lack of national markings on all the aircraft, although one in the background is carrying a small piece of nose art. This is the detachment based at Atsugi, Japan. (Lockheed Martin)

ARS RECEPTACLE

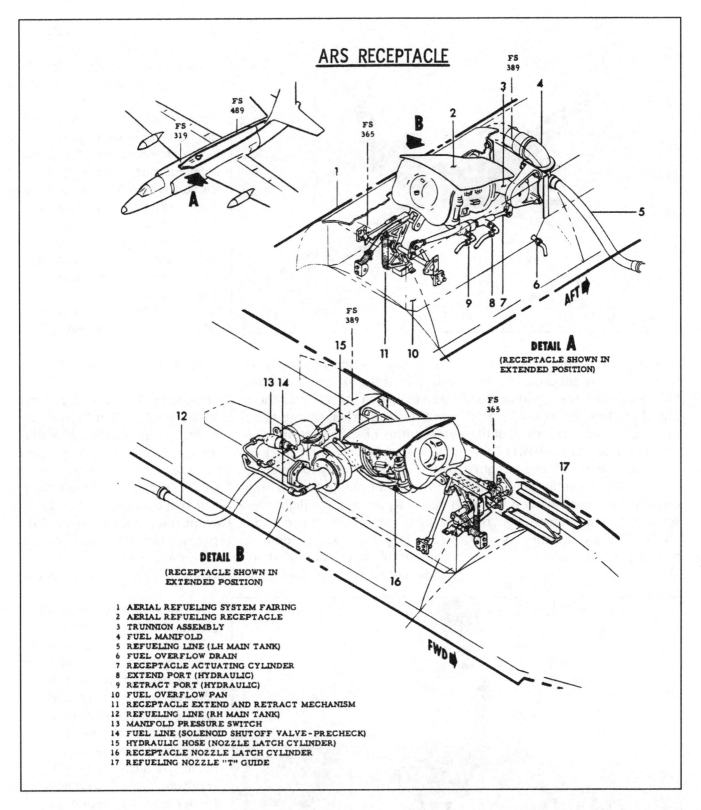

DETAIL A
(RECEPTACLE SHOWN IN
EXTENDED POSITION)

DETAIL B
(RECEPTACLE SHOWN IN
EXTENDED POSITION)

1 AERIAL REFUELING SYSTEM FAIRING
2 AERIAL REFUELING RECEPTACLE
3 TRUNNION ASSEMBLY
4 FUEL MANIFOLD
5 REFUELING LINE (LH MAIN TANK)
6 FUEL OVERFLOW DRAIN
7 RECEPTACLE ACTUATING CYLINDER
8 EXTEND PORT (HYDRAULIC)
9 RETRACT PORT (HYDRAULIC)
10 FUEL OVERFLOW PAN
11 RECEPTACLE EXTEND AND RETRACT MECHANISM
12 REFUELING LINE (RH MAIN TANK)
13 MANIFOLD PRESSURE SWITCH
14 FUEL LINE (SOLENOID SHUTOFF VALVE - PRECHECK)
15 HYDRAULIC HOSE (NOZZLE LATCH CYLINDER)
16 RECEPTACLE NOZZLE LATCH CYLINDER
17 REFUELING NOZZLE "T" GUIDE

An aerial refueling system (ARS) was installed on five small wing U-2s (U-2Es and U-2Fs). This allowed the Dragon Lady to take on as much as 925 gallons of fuel from either a KC-97 or KC-135 tanker. Only the wing tanks could be refueled in flight, not the slipper tanks or drop tanks. Originally the ARS equipment was installed in a small hump or "canoe" on top of the fuselage just ahead of the wing. As more equipment was added to all U-2s this hump grew larger, eventually extending all the way to the vertical stabilizer. The ARS equipment was always located near the front of the hump. (U.S. Air Force)

This was the final configuration for the small-wing U-2s. The "canoe" running along the top of the fuselage housed various electronic systems, and on some aircraft an aerial refueling receptacle. The wing-mounted pods housed fuel or sensors, depending upon the mission. A variety of civilian "N" numbers were used by Lockheed and the CIA, including N809X. The road under the U-2 is Sierra Highway in Palmdale, California. Just out of the photograph to the left is the facility where later U-2s would be manufactured. (Lockheed Martin Skunk Works via Denny Lombard)

of aluminum tubing. The tail surfaces were conventional, with the horizontal stabilizers mounted on top of the fuselage at the base of the vertical stabilizer instead of the tee-tail used on the F-104. In common with many single engine fighters of the era, the entire aft fuselage could be removed for access to the single J57 engine. Interestingly, the aft fuselage was attached by only three 5/8-inch bolts.

The unusual construction was indicative of the extreme measures taken to lighten the airframe. There was a decided lack of stringers and other forms of stiffening, and the skin was only 0.02-inch thick in places. This led directly to extremely low maneuvering limits, only +1.8g/-0.8g under some flight conditions, and never more than +2.5g/-1.0g under any conditions. Compare this to the normal USAF standard of +7.33g/-5.0g for fighter

aircraft of the era.

Bifurcated intakes fed a single Pratt & Whitney J57-P-19 turbojet modified for extreme altitude operations. A special low vapor pressure kerosene fuel was developed by Shell Oil Company, and designated LF-1A by Lockheed and JP-TS by the military. The internal fuel capacity was 1,345 gallons, but an additional 200 gallons could be carried in slipper tanks on the

The Type-A camera installation consisted of three Fairchild HR-732 cameras with 24-inch focal length lenses. Generally, one camera was angled to each side of the aircraft, while the middle camera pointed straight down, although the package could be configured to have all three pointing at nadir. The Type-A configuration carried 1,800 feet of film for each camera, and provided a ground resolution of 2-8 feet. The interchangeable payloads in the Q-bay was a major feature of the U-2 design. (Lockheed Martin Skunk Works via Denny Lombard)

A beautiful natural metal finish U-2C (Article 368, 56-6701) lands at Tucson International Airport on a training flight during December 1968. The large trailing edge flaps are evident here. In the 1960s the Air Force used a leading "0" in the serial number to indicate aircraft over ten years old, and this U-2 obliges by displaying "066701" on the tail. (Mick Roth)

wings or drop tanks under the wings on certain aircraft. The slipper tanks, commonly seen on the later U-2Cs but also carried by some U-2As, attached to each wing leading edge approximately ten feet outboard from the fuselage. The pilot had no indication how much fuel had been used, or remained, from each tank. A simple subtraction-type fuel counter was installed in the cockpit, along with a red warning light that illuminated when 50 gallons remained in the sump tank.

Ahead of the engine was the pressurized "Q-bay" that held the reconnaissance systems. One of the U-2's innovations was that the payloads were attached to interchangeable hatches that could quickly be bolted into the aircraft. A small unpressurized compartment was located in the nose for other payloads, usually small optical cameras. Later, small locations around the tailwheel were used for datalink and ECM systems.

The cockpit was small and cramped

with a single large control wheel similar to that found in most transport aircraft. The instrument panel was largely conventional except for the inclusion of a six-inch hooded driftsight/sextant. The effort to save weight resulted in not providing an ejection seat, and even the deletion of explosive bolts to jettison the canopy. If the pilot needed to bail out, he would have to manually detach the canopy prior to leaving the aircraft. This omission would later prove fatal.

The original small wing U-2s were manufactured in a small facility in Oildale, California, because the Lockheed Burbank plant was too busy filling orders for P2V Neptunes and T-33 trainers. The completed U-2s were partially disassembled and flown to Groom Lake inside C-124 transports. The Oildale facility, located near Bakersfield, had previously built subassemblies for the C-121. The facility was closed shortly after U-2 production was completed. (Lockheed Martin Skunk Works via Denny Lombard)

The Air Force initially flew their U-2s in natural metal finish with standard Air Force markings. This is Article 368 (56-6701) shortly after its delivery in March 1957. The aircraft survived and is currently displayed at the SAC Museum at Offutt AFB as a U-2C. (Lockheed Martin Skunk Works via Denny Lombard)

The optics for the driftsight were located in the top and bottom of the fuselage immediately ahead of the cockpit. A hand control on the right console allowed the pilot to rotate the scope through 360 degrees in azimuth, and to elevate it to an almost horizontal position, thereby gaining complete visual coverage below the aircraft. A switch next to the hand controller provided a 4X magnification mode. The driftsight was the primary navigation device prior to the advent of inertial guidance systems and GPS, and also allowed the pilot to determine the correct location to activate the reconnaissance systems. The driftsight was also frequently used by pilots to determine if missiles or fighters were approaching the aircraft (due to the altitude the U-2 flew at, almost any attack would come from below).

One characteristic of the U-2 airfoil was its very high camber, optimized

At least five early U-2As are visible in the photograph, probably taken at an operating location in England during 1956. Each aircraft carries a fictitious NACA logo and number on the vertical stabilizer. The "sugar scoops" still have not been fitted under the engine exhaust. Noteworthy is the small size of the concrete "hardstands" under each aircraft. (Tony Landis Collection)

One of the U-2C(T) trainers (Article 359, 56-6692) received heavy maintenance at Davis-Monthan in early 1976, and flew a few times without its normal white paint. The addition of the second cockpit did not adversely affect the handling of the aircraft, and provided a much needed conversion and proficiency trainer for the U-2 fleet. (Dennis R. Jenkins via the Mick Roth Collection)

for the best lift/drag ratio at high altitudes. Unfortunately this amplified the airframe's pitching moment, especially at higher airspeeds, and resulted in heavy balancing loads on the horizontal stabilizer. As the initial U-2 pilots would find out, once this balance was upset, the aircraft was only seconds away from breaking up. Johnson solved this problem by providing an innovative "gust control" setting for the wing's trailing edge flaps and ailerons that eliminated the need for structural strengthening, thereby preventing any potential weight penalty. In the gust control setting, the flaps were raised 4° and the ailerons 10° to move the center of pressure forward, compensating for the high camber. Interestingly, a similar feature was proposed for the losing Fairchild BALD EAGLE design, and today is commonplace on most jet transports.

Static engine run-ups were conducted on 27 July, and the first taxi test was conducted on 29 July 1955 by Lockheed test pilot Tony LeVier. This first taxi test was made at 50 knots, and it was noted that the brakes appeared to be weak. The second taxi test was made later the same day, to a speed of 70 knots. While LeVier worked the controls to get an idea of how the aircraft

Lockheed test pilot Bob Schumacher made the first take off from the USS Kitty Hawk (CVA-63) on 4 August 1963. Landing proved a bit more difficult, and Schumacher ended up recovering back to shore when he could not successfully get the U-2 back onto the Kitty Hawk. A small spoiler was added to the top of each wing, solving the problem, although this was not verified until 2 March 1964 when Schumacher landed the aircraft on the USS Ranger (CVA-61). The only operational missions flown from an aircraft carrier were PROJECT SEEKER to monitor French nuclear tests in the South Pacific during May 1964. (Lockheed Martin Skunk Works via the Tony Landis Collection)

Yes, the U-2 could fit in the hanger deck of an aircraft carrier. In 1963 Lockheed conducted trials with a U-2 on the USS Kitty Hawk (CVA-63), resulting in the conversion of three Dragon Ladies to carrier capable U-2Gs. The front landing gear strut was modified to allow it to swivel sideways to accommodate the maneuvering necessary to fit the aircraft through the elevator doors onboard the carrier. The Office of Naval Research (ONR) markings are fictitious. (Lockheed Martin Skunk Works via the Tony Landis Collection)

might behave in flight, he suddenly became aware that he <u>was</u> in flight. The aircraft climbed to an altitude of approximately 35 feet before LeVier could adjust to the flat featureless desert and determine that he had actually left the ground. After some consternation, LeVier managed to get the aircraft back on the ground, although the brakes caught fire and had to be rebuilt.

This incident pointed out the need for reference markings to be painted on the desert – a suggestion LeVier had made weeks before. Another item that LeVier and Johnson had discussed in detail prior to this time was how to land the aircraft. Johnson believed the U-2 should be landed on the main wheels, then lowered onto the tail wheel. LeVier thought it should be stalled-in, with the tail wheel touching down first.

The first intentional flight came at 3:55 pm on 4 August 1955 with Tony LeVier again at the controls. The unpainted aircraft weighed 15,000 pounds at take-off, including the outrigger "pogo" landing struts that had been locked in place for the flight. When the U-2 came in for landing LeVier followed Johnson's instructions and tried to settle down on the main gear. It didn't work. Four more attempts also did not work. Finally, frustrated at these failures, LeVier tried it his way, guiding the U-2 in for a perfect tail-dragger landing using the "gust control" setting to settle the aircraft onto the ground. The most serious problem uncovered was that the brakes were still inadequate. The final solution was a "double" brake system that would be installed on all subsequent U-2s.

Four days later, on 8 August, LeVier made the "official" first flight in front of senior CIA officials. The hour-long flight ended in a reasonable, although still not perfect, landing. To assist in future landings, small fixed strips were added to the wing leading edge just outboard of the fuselage to provide a small measure of stall warning as the air-

Unusual for a photograph taken at Groom Lake, this one still has mountains in the background. All publicly released photographs of the U-2, and its Blackbird successors, had the mountains airbrushed out in an attempt to hide the airstrip's location. Noteworthy on the first Article are the wing-tip skid plates that extend to the trailing edge of the wing. On later aircraft the skid plates terminated at the aileron hinge. (Tony Landis Collection)

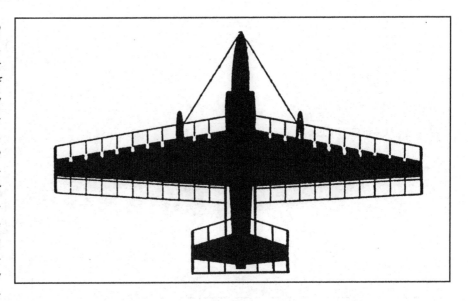

The radar cross section of the U-2 was not considered during its design, mainly because very little thought had been given to the science of radar avoidance. The U-2's primary defense was its high altitude. However, as Soviet air defenses improved, Kelly Johnson began to investigate means to make the U-2 more survivable. One concept, applying radar absorbent foam over the entire outside of the aircraft, resulted in the so-called DIRTY BIRDS. The foam extracted too much of a performance penalty, and was quickly abandoned after the loss of Lockheed test pilot Bob Sieker in Article 341. One of the more bizarre concepts considered was to string wires a quarter-wavelength away from the leading and trailing edge of the wing and tail surfaces. Ideally the return from the wire would cancel out the return from the edge since they were 180° out of phase with each other. Kelly Johnson revealed in 1975 that the flight testing of this configuration achieved "… negligible results in reduction of radar cross section together with the expected adverse aerodynamic effects …" and the idea was dropped. (Mick Roth Collection)

craft drifted over the threshold. Since each aircraft exhibited slightly different flight characteristics, these strips were tailored for individual aircraft

As test flights progressed above Mach 0.85 and 50,000 feet, the pilots were forced to wear uncomfortable S-4/T-1 partial pressure suits – the cockpit was not large enough to accommodate full pressure suits – to protect themselves in case the cockpit unexpectedly depressurized. On 18 October 1955 the U-2 achieved its design altitude of 73,000 feet. When the program's one-year anniversary arrived on 1 December 1955, Lockheed had delivered four aircraft and had five more in the assembly jigs. By the end of the year the aircraft had flown three missions lasting over ten hours (approximately 5,000 miles) and had reached an altitude of 74,500 feet.

The U-2 had some peculiar flight characteristics at altitude. The most worrisome was that the stall speed and never-to-exceed speed could be separated by as little as ten knots. This meant that the aircraft could safely operate in a speed range of only ten knots. In fact, if a pilot turned too sharply, the inside wing could be in "stall buffet" (going too slowly) while the outside wing could be in "Mach buffet" (too fast). Recovery from a stall (too

Kelly Johnson studied armed U-2s almost from the beginning. This wind tunnel model shows seven hard points under each wing, interesting considering the fragile nature of the wing to begin with. Most armed versions used a more conventional tricycle landing gear configuration, with a nose gear in the fuselage where the main gear was normally located, and new main gear in mid-wing pods. (Lockheed Martin Skunk Works via the Tony Landis Collection)

The Special Projects Branch at the Air Force Flight Test Center at Edwards operated several U-2s. Article 389 (56-6722), in the foreground, was equipped with a turret containing a spectrometer to gather radiation background information for the MIDAS satellite program. Although similar in appearance to the SMOKEY JOE aircraft, this was a single seater, and the turret contained a different sensor suite. The forward top half of the aircraft was painted black to prevent reflections from interfering with the sensor. Article 368 (56-6701) is in the background. (U.S. Air Force via the Tony Landis Collection)

slow) could be difficult since elevator authority was limited, while exceeding the maximum permissible speed by as little as four knots could result in the aircraft breaking up. In order to assist the pilots, Lockheed provided a fairly effective autopilot, but it was still incumbent on the pilot to ensure the aircraft was in the proper speed regime. Luckily, as fuel was burned the margin for error increased, so as a pilot tired on a long flight he actually had more latitude for mistakes.

Flameouts were a frequent occurrence during the early flight test program. This was not a pleasant event at 65,000 feet, since the U-2 had to descend to 35,000 feet or lower in order to effect an air start. Luckily, the U-2 could glide some

The Target Radiation Intensity Measurement (TRIM) project used Article 359 (56-6692) for three years beginning in 1971. Two tracking sensors in rotating domes were installed, one above the Q-bay and one about half-way to the tail. These sensors measured the radiation characteristics of reentry vehicles as part of a ballistic missile defense project. This aircraft is now configured as a U-2C and displayed at RAF Alconbury, England. (Lockheed Martin Skunk Works via the Tony Landis Collection)

The first U-2D (Article 388, 56-6721) displays an assortment of photo-reference markings on its vertical stabilizer and wings. The second cockpit canopy opened differently from the front canopy. The two U-2Ds were used extensively for testing the MIDAS infrared sensor. Typical missions involved monitoring the rocket plumes of Intercontinental Ballistic Missiles (ICBM) launched from either Vandenberg AFB or Cape Canaveral AFS from a location approximately 200 miles down-range at an altitude of 60,000 feet. (U.S. Air Force via the Tony Landis Collection)

275 miles, taking some 73 minutes to do so. The interim J57-P-37 engine also had the undesirable habit of dumping engine oil into the cockpit ventilation system, allowing a greasy black film to accumulate on everything, including the windscreen. Some U-2 test pilots began to carry rags attached to long sticks in order to clean the windscreen!

Strangely, the developed high-altitude version of the Pratt & Whitney engine was designated J57-P-31, numerically lower than the interim -37 unit. This was because work had begun on the final version before it became apparent that the development would not be complete in time to support the U-2 flight test program. The interim version was therefore begun after the final version, hence the later number. Also,

One of the U-2Ds (Article 394, 56-6954) assigned to Edwards AFB. A second seat was installed in the Q-bay, allowing an engineer to be flown to monitor or control experiments. The second seat was not equipped with flight controls, and contained only very basic flight instrumentation and an ejection seat. Although not shown here, the SMOKEY JOE two-seat U-2Ds carried the MIDAS infrared sensor in a turret between projecting upward between the two cockpits. The fairing shown here over the second cockpit, along with the unusual paint scheme, indicates this U-2D had probably carried the MIDAS experiment recently. (Tony Landis Collection)

Two of the Air Force Flight Test Center's U-2s fly over the Edwards' flightline. The closest aircraft is Article 368 (56-6701) which was later retired to the SAC Museum at Offutt AFB. The aircraft in the background is Article 389 (56-6722) configured with a turret containing sensors as part of the MIDAS satellite program. It was later retired to the Air Force Museum at Wright-Patterson AFB, Ohio, where it was reconfigured as a U-2A. (U.S. Air Force via the Tony Landis Collection)

This was the first official picture of the U-2 released to the public. It shows the aircraft in NACA markings, and identified it as a "weather research airplane." In truth most early U-2 flights did carry NACA instruments, and most of the data from those instruments was eventually turned over to the NACA. The clean airframe of the early U-2As would later be adorned with a variety of scoops and antennas as more systems were added. (Lockheed Martin)

both the -31 and the -37 were derivatives of the -19, which powered some early aircraft not intended to operate at high altitudes. The final -31 engines would provide 11,200 lbf take-off thrust at sea level, a useful 700 pound increase over the -37.

During May 1951, a special study group codenamed BEACON HILL met to discuss aerial reconnaissance systems. The modified bombers previously used as reconnaissance platforms had been able to accommodate exceptionally large cameras. By the end of World War II, Harvard University had

Article 389 (56-6722) is amongst the most photographed of the small wing U-2s, mostly because it was used fairly openly by the Air Force Flight Test Center at Edwards. It also wore a variety of paint schemes, this one being overall black, but with the Air Force markings typically seen on natural metal aircraft of the time period. The small hump on the fuselage at the wing leading edge houses the HF radio tuner. Later, this hump would extended all the way to the vertical stabilizer as more

systems were added to the aircraft. The long gust sensing probe projecting from the nose was part of the High-altitude Clear Air Turbulence (HiCAT) test program. (Lockheed Martin)

developed a 100-inch focal length (the distance between the outer lens and the film) camera that was capable of looking sideways into enemy territory 100 miles away; and the RB-36 bomber was capable of carrying a 240-inch focal length unit that was over 14 feet high! The success of the U-2, however, would depend upon much smaller units in order to fit into the aircraft.

Technology, however, was evolving rapidly. Eastman Kodak had developed new films that provided clearer images on a thinner substrate, decreasing the size and weight of the film package. Computers allowed the design of mirrors with more efficient folding optics. By late 1954 the BEACON HILL group had defined three types of cameras: Type-A units were standard cameras (i.e., KA-1, K-38, etc.) that were already in the Air Force inventory, although they were refurbished and optimized for better precision; the new Type-B had a 36-inch focal length; the Type-C camera, not completed until well into the initial U-2 operations, had a 180-inch focal length using a complicated series of folded optics. The Type-C camera proved to be "too much" and was not extensively used.

This left the Type-B camera to conduct most of the early U-2 surveillance. The 400 pound camera used two 9.5-inch film strips moving in opposite directions to keep the aircraft's center of gravity constant while the camera operated The two 9.5-inch strips provided an 18x18-inch image using thin-base film on two 6,500-foot rolls, providing approximately 4,000 pairs of images. The standard 36-inch focal length lens had an aperture of f/8 and ultimately provided a ground

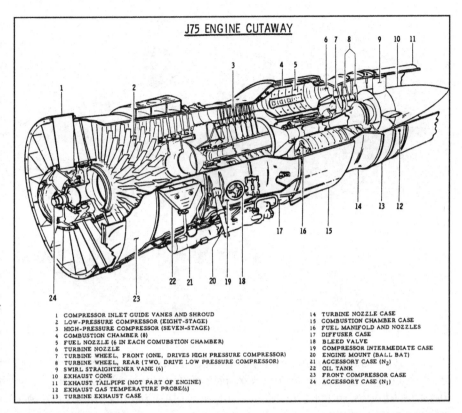

J75 ENGINE CUTAWAY

1 COMPRESSOR INLET GUIDE VANES AND SHROUD
2 LOW-PRESSURE COMPRESSOR (EIGHT-STAGE)
3 HIGH-PRESSURE COMPRESSOR (SEVEN-STAGE)
4 COMBUSTION CHAMBER (8)
5 FUEL NOZZLE (6 IN EACH COMUBSTION CHAMBER)
6 TURBINE NOZZLE
7 TURBINE WHEEL, FRONT (ONE, DRIVES HIGH PRESSURE COMPRESSOR)
8 TURBINE WHEEL, REAR (TWO, DRIVE LOW PRESSURE COMPRESSOR)
9 SWIRL STRAIGHTENER VANE (6)
10 EXHAUST CONE
11 EXHAUST TAILPIPE (NOT PART OF ENGINE)
12 EXHAUST GAS TEMPERATURE PROBE(6)
13 TURBINE EXHAUST CASE
14 TURBINE NOZZLE CASE
15 COMBUSTION CHAMBER CASE
16 FUEL MANIFOLD AND NOZZLES
17 DIFFUSER CASE
18 BLEED VALVE
19 COMPRESSOR INTERMEDIATE CASE
20 ENGINE MOUNT (BALL BAT)
21 ACCESSORY CASE (N_2)
22 OIL TANK
23 FRONT COMPRESSOR CASE
24 ACCESSORY CASE (N_1)

The J75 engine used in the U-2 was a high-altitude derivative of the engine used in the F-105 and F-106 fighter aircraft. It was an advanced and powerful engine for its day, and Pratt & Whitney adapted it to the high altitude U-2 without too much difficulty, something that could not be said of the trials and tribulations surrounding the development of the high altitude version of the earlier J57. (U.S. Air Force)

resolution of 12 inches (initial resolution is quoted at 30 inches, but improved as better film and lenses became available). Actual operational reliability of the camera proved to be 98%, completing over 10 million in-flight cycles.

In addition to the Type-B camera, most early U-2 flights also carried a 35mm tracker camera that continuously scanned from horizon-to-horizon to provide photo-interpreters an accurate track of the aircraft's flight path. Despite its relatively small payload capability, a surprising amount of signals intelligence (SIGINT), electronic intelligence (ELINT), and communications intelligence (COMINT) equipment, found its way onto the U-2

fleet over the years. Much of this was supplied by the Air Force, or was modified by the CIA from Air Force equipment. However, Ramo-Woolridge (now TRW) developed many specialized systems for the U-2s. This equipment was squeezed into the nose, locations in the Q-bay, beneath the cockpit side consoles, and in small compartments aft of the engine intakes and around the tail wheel. Since the U-2 pilot had his hands full flying the aircraft and operating the camera equipment, the electronics usually operated automatically based on time. Unlike the complex Air Force alphanumeric designation system, the CIA used a simple numeric sequence, with the first installation being called "System 1" – by the

The early U-2s had an extremely cramped cockpit, limiting the pilots to wearing a partial pressure suit. Here Francis Gary Powers, long before he became famous, models the MC-3A suit and MA-2 helmet, minus the face plate. A nomex flight suit was worn over this pressure suit to protect it from fire and also to eliminate the chances of the laces or capstans getting tangled on something in the cockpit. (Lockheed Martin)

1990, System 30 was operational (there was also a System 192 – no reference to Systems 31-191 was found).

In December 1955 Lockheed received the go-ahead for a further 30 production aircraft, bringing the total to 50. Again, Johnson managed to underrun the contract, and returned almost $2 million to the Government. After production was completed, a further five aircraft were built mostly from spare parts, with only some minor systems (and engines) being funded anew. Interestingly, most of the U-2s were not built at the Lockheed plant in Burbank. The main plant was busy building P2V Neptune anti-submarine aircraft for the Navy and T-33 trainers for the Air Force, so U-2 production was set up in a building 90 miles north of Burbank in Oildale, just outside Bakersfield, that had originally built subassemblies for the C-121 transport. The plant began constructing U-2s in January 1956, and by the end of the year there were 400 people, mainly local laborers, working there. The U-2s were completely assembled and checked-out inside the building at Oildale, then partially disassembled and trucked to the local airport for transport to Groom Lake inside C-124s. By the end of 1957 the plant was closed and U-2 production was complete – at least for the time being.

Article 388 (56-6721) carried a SMOKEY JOE emblem on the vertical stabilizer during its MIDAS test program. The rotating turret between the cockpits housed a sensitive infrared sensor to detect ballistic missile launches. The turret could rotate 180° horizontally, and the sensor contained within it could elevate 30° above the aircraft's flight path. The MIDAS program ran into numerous technical problems, notably a decided lack of information on natural background radiation, which caused several other U-2s to be enlisted to measure background radiation to serve as a baseline for the project. SMOKEY JOE missions were flown from Edwards (supporting Vandenberg launches), as well as Patrick AFB, Florida, and Ramey AFB, Puerto Rico (to support launches from Cape Canaveral). (Lockheed Martin)

In mid-1957 the Air Force began receiving some U-2s from the second production lot. These were essentially identical to the CIA aircraft, although they would begin to diverge in both equipment and capabilities almost immediately as each organization added their own sensors and electronic systems.

By now operational missions were being flown on a routine basis, and the ability of the Soviets to track the U-2 was alarming to all concerned. Lockheed began investigating means to reduce the U-2's radar signature, and Kelly Johnson developed various concepts, some of which were quite fantastic and of questionable value. Perhaps the most bizarre was one to string wires of various lengths between the fuselage, wings, and tail in order to scatter the radar energy in different directions. The idea which was finally flight tested involved wrapping the entire airframe with a metallic grid known as SALISBURY SCREEN which was covered by a microwave absorbent ECHOSORB coating made of foam rubber. The resulting aircraft were often referred to as DIRTY BIRDs, and were almost universally disliked by pilots for their degraded handling qualities. However, none of the materials proved effective across the entire spectrum of Soviet radar frequencies, and all extracted a considerable penalty on aircraft performance. The coatings also prevented the dissipation of heat from the engine through the aircraft skin. During a DIRTY BIRD test flight with the U-2 prototype (Article 341), Bob Sieker experienced a flameout at 72,000 feet due to heat build-up caused by the foam coating. Unfortunately Sieker's pressure suit faceplate failed and he suffocated before the U-2 crashed in the desert.

This was the configuration flown on most late CIA U-2 missions. This is a J75-powered aircraft with intermediate-sized air intakes. Later in life the intakes would grow slightly in size to allow more air into the engine. The original 90° "sugar scoop" is seen under the exhaust. The small hump on the top of the fuselage houses HF radio equipment and part of the System 9 ECM equipment. The aircraft is finished in midnight blue paint with no national insignia. The civilian "N" number would be removed once the aircraft left the United States. (Lockheed Martin)

Further analysis by Johnson indicated that the only effective way of producing a smaller radar cross-section was to design an aircraft with that objective from the beginning – and gave birth to the A-12/SR-71 program. About the only thing that could be done for the U-2 was to paint it in such a way as to provide a small measure against being visually detected by fighters attempting to intercept during an overflight. Originally, all Air Force U-2s were left in their natural metal finish. In 1961-62 they were repainted in a high-gloss light grey. Various schemes, including polka dots and zebra stripes, were flight tested over Edwards, but none proved terribly effective. The CIA decided to paint their aircraft a very dark "midnight blue" since it would blend into the dark sky that is prevalent at high altitude, and the Air Force began to follow in 1964. In many photographs this particular shade of blue takes an an almost glossy sheen. In 1965 the Air Force introduced the BLACK VELVET paint scheme that used an extremely flat black paint, and by 1966 all Air Force and CIA aircraft had been repainted.

By March 1963, 21 of the original 55 U-2s had been lost, mainly to accidents, but also to combat losses. Kelly Johnson suggested building 25 additional aircraft at a cost of approximately $25 million. The CIA was not particularly interested since most of its money was being invested in Johnson's A-12 project, and the Air Force was busy with the RB-57F which could carry a significantly larger payload than the U-2. This ultimate big-wing B-57 variant would not live up to its expectations, never realizing its performance goals and being something of a maintenance nightmare in operations. The A-12, while a technical triumph, would fly fewer than 30 operational missions before being retired.

At the beginning of U-2 development, Johnson and the CIA realized that Soviet air defenses would eventually catch up with the aircraft. At the time it was estimated the U-2 would be relatively invulnerable to Soviet defenses for approximately two years, after which it was much more likely aircraft could be lost. By 1958 the

The U-2F added an aerial refueling capability to the basic U-2C configuration. The dorsal hump was extended to house the refueling receptacle as well as the HF radio and System 9 equipment. Most CIA U-2s kept their white sun shield over the canopy, although later in their careers the Air Force U-2s would get black sunshades. The lighter lines on top of the wings indicate walkways for the maintenance crew. (Lockheed Martin)

Soviets were beginning to deploy the new SA-2 GUIDELINE surface-to-air missile (SAM) with its FAN SONG radar. This weapon, as would later be demonstrated, would be capable of attacking the U-2A, although with a rather dismal 2% probability of kill.

Electronic countermeasures (ECM) equipment to combat the SA-2, as well as an ever-increasing quantity of sensors, began to take a toll on the U-2As performance. The BLACK VELVET paint had added 80 pounds, while ECM equipment added 30 more. An ejection seat and other safety equipment added another 100 pounds. This had reduced the aircraft's weight margin to nearly zero. In response Lockheed began to develop an improved version of the Dragon Lady, the re-engined U-2C.

The Pratt & Whitney J75 engine was essentially a modernized version of the J57, and produced 15,800 lbf, a 4,600 lbf increase. The J75 was slightly larger in diameter and several feet longer than the J57, but still fit within the U-2's fuselage. Unfortunately, the engine weighed 750 pounds more, upsetting the U-2's already delicate center-of-gravity and putting further strains on the horizontal stabilizer. The stabilizer was replaced with one of revised camber, but the c.g. range of the U-2C were even tighter than the U-2A – only 1.5 inches. As a result, the margin between stall buffet and Mach buffet decreased to only four knots in some flight regimes. Ballast in the tail was used to balance the aircraft, with even the individual pilot's weight making a difference.

The final J75-P-13B high altitude version produced 17,000 lbf at sea level, and high altitude output had improved to almost 10%. By substituting the J75 engine in place of the J57, the U-2C could almost match the original performance of the U-2A. Five aircraft were converted during 1958 with the new engines, larger intakes, and various improved systems. The new altitude capability came at a cost, how-

A beautiful shot of a U-2A Article 382 (56-6715) shows why the aircraft was usually compared to a glider. The flaps, elevators, and rudder of this aircraft have been painted a bright red contrasting with its natural metal finish. The 80-foot span high-aspect ratio wing used three main spars, but substituted a lattice-work of aluminum tubing for more conventional ribs. The resulting wing was rather fragile. (Lockheed Martin)

ever, and the maximum range of the U-2C was approximately 500 miles less than the U-2A. The U-2C's maximum gross weight of 24,000 pounds was 7,000 pounds greater than the original U-2A.

And the extra thrust let the U-2 climb like a fighter. At less than gross weight, the U-2C could climb to 30,000 feet in less than four minutes. At maximum weight the aircraft could still climb to 67,000 feet in less than 50 minutes, covering less than 300 miles of ground track. In fact, one of the operating characteristics of the U-2 was its almost vertical climb immediately after take-off, a maneuver designed to minimize stress on the horizontal stabilizer. The U-2 climbs quickly to 50,000 feet where it enters a gradual cruise climb for the rest of the flight, ascending as fuel is burned off to 70,000 feet or above. The numbers vary depending on the mission weight, range required, outside air temperature and other factors. When it is time to return, speedbrakes and landing gear are deployed, since the U-2 will not voluntarily leave altitude until "the engine quits". Contrary to popular misconception, U-2 pilots never turn off the engine and glide to increase the range.

There were nine versions of the basic U-2 allocated official designations, beginning with the initial 53 production U-2A-1-LOs. With the exception of the two purpose-built U-2D aircraft, all subsequent small-wing U-2s were converted from one of these aircraft.

Five modified WU-2A-1-LOs (Articles 381-385) had dedicated gas and particulate sampling systems installed in the Q-bay and a "hard nose" containing a small intake

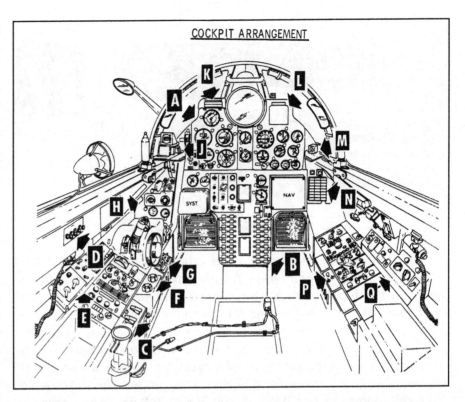

The general cockpit arrangement of the U-2C and U-2F were similar, the primary difference being the relocation of the System 12B ECM display (at item "L") from the U-2F in order to accommodate the controls and indicators for the aerial refueling system. The System 12B display was moved to a location denoted by "N". (U.S. Air Force)

valve assembly for the sampling mission. Some sources list these aircraft as U-2A-2-LOs.

The U-2B was a proposed bomber version of the Dragon Lady. These aircraft were to be equipped with a tricycle landing gear with the nose gear located in the normal main gear location in the fuselage and the new forward retracting main gear located in large wing pods. Two hard-points would be located under each wing, and a single M60 gun would be carried on a trapeze located in the Q-bay for self defense. Other variations of this concept would be considered over the years, including ones using the larger U-2R airframe, but none ever made it past paper studies and wind tunnel testing. There were numerous other proposals for U-2

variants that were not proceeded with. For instance, in December 1964 Johnson proposed a tanker based on the U-2 airframe that could refuel other U-2s at 70,000 feet.

Over the years, all surviving U-2As were converted to the U-2C-1-LO standard. This included the more powerful J75 engine and larger air intakes, as well as various improved equipment. The first aircraft (Article 342) converted made its first flight in the new configuration on 13 May 1959. Two other aircraft (351 and 358) were also used during the U-2C test program, which lasted 106 flights covering slightly over 381 flight hours.

The two purpose-built U-2D-1-LO aircraft (388 and 394) were unique

One of the most public missions undertaken by the early U-2s was the High-Altitude Sampling Program (HASP) effort. Although most early missions were flown with a "hard nose" containing a sampling unit, later missions used an F-2/P-3 sampling system fitted into the Q-bay. A series of paper filters could be extended into the scoop under the Q-bay to capture particulate matter, such as that released from air-burst nuclear weapon tests. In addition, atmosphere samples could be taken and stored in six bottles in the Q-bay for further analysis on the ground. This is Article 363 (56-6696) configured for a HASP mission. The aircraft would later take part in overflights during the Cuban missile crisis. (Lockheed Martin)

in being the only production two seat versions of the small-wing U-2. With the exception of the second seat in the Q-bay location, these were essentially identical to early U-2As and were powered by J57 engines throughout their careers.

Three U-2As (Articles 347, 354, and 355) were equipped with flying-boom aerial refueling systems and

redesignated U-2E-1-LO. Kelly Johnson had originally proposed the idea of fitting the U-2 with refueling receptacles in June 1960 and an initial test was conducted in October by flying a U-2 in close proximity to a KC-135 tanker to determine the aerodynamic interaction between the two aircraft. Final approval for the modifications came the following May. Two U-2Cs

(Articles 370 and 374) were equipped with aerial refueling systems and redesignated U-2F-1-LO. The three U-2Es were also redesignated U-2F-1-LO when they were re-engined with J75s, making a total of five U-2Fs.

In one of the more interesting conversions, three U-2Cs (348, 349, and 362) were equipped with arresting hooks and other specialized equipment and redesignated U-2G-1-LO. Lockheed was asked in May 1963 to study using a U-2 for naval operations, and in July a CIA U-2A was modified by adding three longerons to the aft fuselage, a faired tail hook ahead of the tail wheel, and cable guards in front of the main wheels. The main landing gear strut was also modified to allow it to swivel sideways to ease maneuvering around the carrier's elevators and hanger deck.

On 4 August 1963 a U-2G was flown from North Edwards to NAS North Island and loaded aboard the USS Kitty Hawk (CVA-63). During the following trials, the U-2 was flown by Lockheed test pilot Bob Schumacher and took off in 321 feet with the carrier making 24 knots into a 6 knot wind. The U-2 was not capable of catapult launches. Landing proved to be a bit more problematic, and after three unsuccessful approaches, Schumacher flew back to North Edwards. Johnson believed the problem was solvable and added a small spoiler on the top of each wing, along with cable guards on the wing tips. Schumacher flew the modified aircraft to the USS Ranger (CVA-61) on 2 March 1964 and landed successfully. This was followed by two days of familiarization flights by several other Lockheed and CIA pilots. Two further aircraft were modified, and

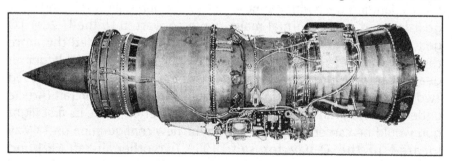

The Pratt & Whitney J57-P-31 was initially used in all small wing U-2s. This was a high altitude variant of the engine used in the B-52 and early Century-series fighters. Although the engine proved troublesome at first, it matured into a good, dependable powerplant for the U-2, and was replaced with the later J75 simply because the U-2's weight had grown beyond the engines power capabilities. (Pratt & Whitney)

all three U-2Gs were turned over to the CIA which trained a half-dozen pilots on carrier landing techniques. During these tests the aircraft were assigned civil registrations (N315X, N801X, and N808X) and carried Office of Naval Research markings on the vertical stabilizers.

The timing proved to be ideal. In May 1964 the French were ready to test their nuclear bomb at Mururoa in the South Pacific. Since there were no land bases that provided convenient access for the high altitude sampling missions, a single U-2G was loaded aboard Ranger under PROJECT SEEKER. This aircraft provided valuable intelligence during the French tests, but this was the only known operational use of carrier based U-2s.

A further modification of the U-2G, the single U-2H-1-LO was a carrier-equipped U-2C that was also equipped for aerial refueling. All of this extra equipment had a somewhat adverse effect on the aircraft's performance, and it spent most of its time at North Edwards being used for training and equipment testing.

The DIRTY BIRD program was an attempt to create a stealth U-2, long before the term was in widespread use. The entire bottom of the U-2 was covered in ECHOSORB, a radar absorbing foam sheet that covered a SALISBURY SCREEN metallic mesh. Unfortunately, ECHOSORB was much better at keeping heat in the aircraft than it was at absorbing radar signals. All of the attempts to make a stealth U-2 failed, and indirectly gave birth to the Lockheed Blackbird project. (Lockheed Martin Skunk Works)

An alarming rate of pilot attrition during flight training demonstrated the need for a two-seat version of the U-2. Two airframes (Articles 359 and 393) were modified with a raised second cockpit on top of the Q-bay and used for pilot familiarization. These U-2C(T)-1-LOs were not considered operationally capable. Interestingly, these were the longest surviving small-wing U-2s, serving the Air Force until U-2R trainers were available from the last production run in the 1980s.

Project HiCAT (High-altitude Clear Air Turbulence) used a long gust vane protruding from the nose of the U-2. This was one of the earliest studies into clear air turbulence, a problem which still largely avoids detection with resultant damage to unsuspecting aircraft. The concept of flying the fragile U-2, with its known handling limitations, into areas of suspected turbulence shows the character of test pilots. The round glass object behind the base of the gust vane is the optics for the driftscope. (U.S. Air Force)

EARLY U-2 OPERATIONS

DRAGONS OVER RUSSIA AND CHINA

The Dragon Lady had been designated U-2 to disguise its actual mission ("U" is usually reserved for converted civil light aircraft – Pipers, Cessnas, etc.). Two different cover stories emerged. Unbelievably, the first indicated that the U-2 (and it was always referred to as a singular entity) was a test vehicle to examine certain flight characteristics relative to the F-104 program. The second story was that the aircraft was used by the National Advisory Committee for Aeronautics (NACA) for high altitude atmospheric and weather research. In fact, when the U-2 was first unveiled to the public it carried fictitious NACA markings,

something that was repeated many times over the early years of the program.

The NACA deception, reluctantly agreed to by NACA boss Hugh L. Dryden, was not totally false. The cover story was that the aircraft were being used to collect information on the jet stream, cosmic ray particles, ozone, etc., and most early U-2 training flights around the world did carry NACA instruments. The data was turned over to the NACA for evaluation, but the pilots were always CIA cum Lockheed, and the NACA had no say-so in where or when the data was collected.

During early 1956, the first group of six CIA pilots arrived at Groom Lake as part of OPERATION OVER-FLIGHT. These were active duty military pilots who had been "sanitized" by the CIA – their names and backgrounds were fictitious, and officially they were employed by Lockheed, although their pay came from CIA funds. The flight training program itself proved to be relatively straight forward, right up until landing. Landing the U-2 would always be problematic, especially for pilots that had never flown tail-draggers. Nevertheless, by the beginning of summer, all six pilots had successfully completed their training and ten U-2As were available for operations. It was time to use the Dragon Lady.

On 30 April 1956, two U-2s were disassembled and transported to RAF Lakenheath where the first of three CIA detachments was formed, this one known as the 1st Weather Reconnaissance Squadron, Provisional (WRSP-1). To the pilots and Lockheed

When the U-2Cs went back to England in the 1970s, the British requested that they not be painted black. Instead of simply restoring them to their former natural metal or light grey finish, the Air Force selected a two-tone grey camouflage. The majority of missions flown in this paint scheme were dedicated to testing the Advanced Location Strike System (ALSS), a predecessor to the Precision Location and Strike System (PLSS) developed for the TR-1A. Neither system was developed far enough to be operationally fielded. This is Article 359 (56-6692) which is currently on display at RAF Alconbury. (Lockheed Martin Skunk Works via Denny Lombard)

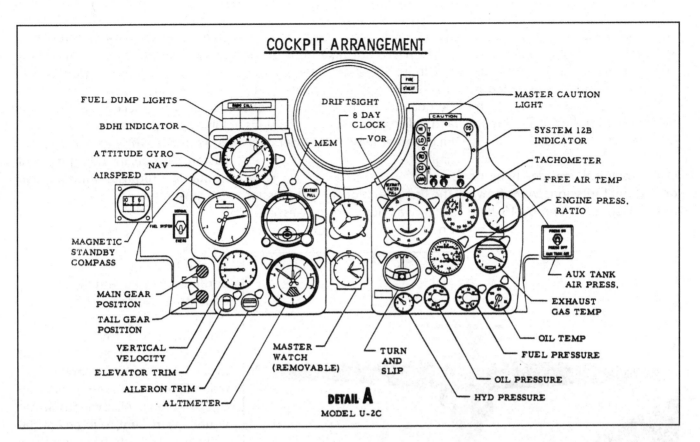

COCKPIT ARRANGEMENT

FUEL DUMP LIGHTS
BDHI INDICATOR
ATTITUDE GYRO
NAV
AIRSPEED

MAGNETIC STANDBY COMPASS

MAIN GEAR POSITION
TAIL GEAR POSITION
VERTICAL VELOCITY
ELEVATOR TRIM
AILERON TRIM
ALTIMETER

DRIFTSIGHT
8 DAY CLOCK
MEM
VOR

MASTER WATCH (REMOVABLE)
TURN AND SLIP

MASTER CAUTION LIGHT
SYSTEM 12B INDICATOR
TACHOMETER
FREE AIR TEMP
ENGINE PRESS. RATIO

AUX TANK AIR PRESS.
EXHAUST GAS TEMP
OIL TEMP
FUEL PRESSURE
OIL PRESSURE
HYD PRESSURE

DETAIL A
MODEL U-2C

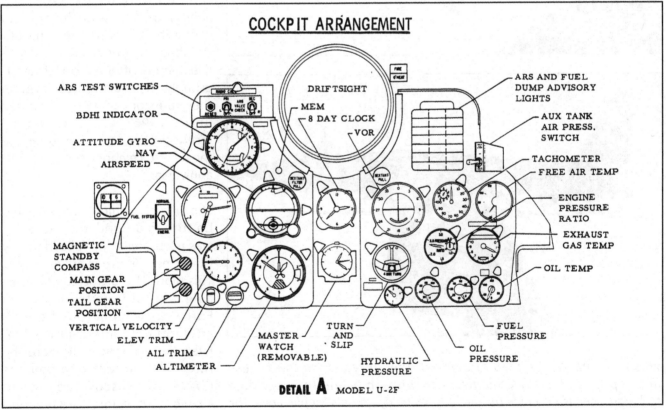

COCKPIT ARRANGEMENT

ARS TEST SWITCHES
BDHI INDICATOR
ATTITUDE GYRO
NAV
AIRSPEED

MAGNETIC STANDBY COMPASS
MAIN GEAR POSITION
TAIL GEAR POSITION
VERTICAL VELOCITY
ELEV TRIM
AIL TRIM
ALTIMETER

DRIFTSIGHT
MEM
8 DAY CLOCK
VOR

MASTER WATCH (REMOVABLE)
TURN AND SLIP
HYDRAULIC PRESSURE

ARS AND FUEL DUMP ADVISORY LIGHTS
AUX TANK AIR PRESS. SWITCH
TACHOMETER
FREE AIR TEMP
ENGINE PRESSURE RATIO
EXHAUST GAS TEMP
OIL TEMP

FUEL PRESSURE
OIL PRESSURE

DETAIL A MODEL U-2F

The primary difference between the U-2C and U-2F cockpits was the relocation of the System 12B display from the upper right, and its replacement with the controls and displays necessary to operate the aerial refueling system. The System 12B display was moved to a position further right, off the main instrument panel proper. (U.S. Air Force)

personnel, it was simply "Det A" and although technically a CIA operation, almost all logistics and maintenance support was provided by the Air Force and Lockheed. The first U-2 flight from Lakenheath occurred on 21 May 1956.

Due to political considerations, no operational missions were flown from Lakenheath, and on 15 June Det A moved to the American air base at Wiesbaden, Germany. The British were not taken out of the U-2 loop, however; in fact, during May 1958 four British pilots would be qualified to fly U-2 operations and did so on numerous occasions, including at least two Soviet overflights.

The first operational flight (mission 2003) was flown from Wiesbaden on 20 June 1956 by CIA pilot Carl Overstreet embarking over Warsaw, the Prague, and a bit of East Germany. The photography was excellent, and it appeared the Soviets had not tracked the U-2. On 2 July two separate flights (missions 2009 and 2010) were flown over Eastern Europe, including most of Rumania, Bulgaria, Hungary, and Czechoslovakia.

This is Skunk Works' idea of camouflage! In response to Chinese interceptions of U-2 overflights, Kelly Johnson began to investigate techniques to visually hide the aircraft. White "polka dots" applied over the midnight blue paint did not prove to be effective, although the black sunshade pioneered here was adopted. The BLACK VELVET paint scheme, not much different than the midnight blue, was an outgrowth of this effort. (Lockheed Martin Skunk Works via Denny Lombard)

Two days later, Harvey Stockman took the U-2 over the Soviet Union for the first time, flying over East Berlin, across Poland via Poznan, and into Belorussia as far as Minsk before heading over Leningrad, Estonia, Latvia, and Lithuania. Whereas Overstreet's flight had gone largely unnoticed, Stockman's flight was carefully followed by Soviet radar. Also, various Soviet fighters were sent to intercept the U-2 and were clearly visible to Stockman through the ventral driftsight. Stockman returned to Wiesbaden eight hours and forty-five minutes after he had left. Interestingly, the exact routes flown on these missions remained classified until 1996 when Lockheed received CIA permission to release the data to celebrate the U-2's 40th anniversary.

Showing how quickly the U-2 could be turned around, the same U-2 was used again the following day by Carmen Vito to overfly Moscow. This flight also attracted considerable interest from the Soviet Air Force, with numerous fighters attempting to intercept the U-2. Even more threatening were the three SA-1 surface-to-air missile (SAM) sites discovered around Moscow. Although the sites were not yet completed, and the photography provided valuable data on the possible characteristics of the first operational Soviet SAMs, the

fact that they existed spelled the beginning of the end for the U-2 overflights.

On 10 July 1956 the Soviet Union lodged a diplomatic complaint regarding the overflights by a "… twin-engined U.S. Air Force aircraft …". The State Department denied that any U.S. military aircraft had violated Soviet airspace. This was, technically, the truth. The U-2s were officially private aircraft, owned and operated by Lockheed under contract to the CIA, which was a civilian agency. And they were not twin-engined. Although the ideal response to a lawyer, it is unlikely that it either calmed or amused the Soviets. In order to prevent any future diplomatic incidents, President Eisenhower directed that all future overflights of Soviet territory receive his personal approval.

After each U-2 flight the film would be removed, developed, and duplicated at the landing site. The copy would be retained locally as a contingency, while the original negatives were taken by courier aircraft to Washington, D.C. for evaluation. This "photo interpretation" took place in a converted garage (codenamed AUTOMAT) in a not-too-good neighborhood in Washington by a group that eventually numbered over 1,000 people. After it was all processed, enlarged, and printed, each mission produced sufficient material to cover the entire Baltimore-Washington turnpike!

Forty years after the events, the CIA finally declassified the routes taken by the first three operational U-2 missions over Europe. The first mission (2003) was flown by CIA pilot Carl Overstreet on 20 June 1956. Two more missions were flown on 2 July 1956. None of these ventured over the Soviet Union. (Lockheed Martin Skunk Works via Denny Lombard)

In May 1956 the second CIA pilot class entered training at Groom Lake, completing the course in August. Shortly thereafter "Det B" was formed at Incirlik, Turkey, with approximately 100 CIA and Lockheed personnel, plus limited Air Force support for weather forecasting and flight planning. Seven pilots, including one named Gary Francis Powers, and five U-2As were assigned to the detachment. Early in 1957 the original Det A was moved from Wiesbaden to a remote airfield at Giebelstadt, but the political climate in Europe was still not favorable and the detachment was merged with Det B at Incirlik by the end of the year. After the last CIA pilot class finished their training in 1957, the third detachment, "Det C", was formed at Atsugi, Japan.

A total of six U-2s were modified for aerial refueling. Three U-2As were so equipped, becoming U-2Es and two U-2Cs were also modified, becoming U-2Fs in the process. The three U-2Es also became U-2Fs when they were re-engined with the J75. A single U-2H was a modification of the U-2C that was both aerial refuelable and carrier capable. The U-2 could be refueled by either KC-97 or KC-135 tankers. (U.S. Air Force via the Tony Landis Collection)

By the end of its fourth year in operation, the CIA considered the U-2 to be the single most important technical intelligence gathering means in the inventory. U-2 flights had revealed the fallacy of the Soviet jet bomber threat; the true number of of Soviet ICBMs; and had underscored the shortcomings of Soviet technology in general. However, it was an understanding based on a very limited sample.

In the 48 month period ending in December 1960, only 40 excursions over Soviet territory had been completed by OPERATION OVERFLIGHT. In addition to excellent photography, these missions also deployed the PURPLE FLASH seismic sensor system around the Soviet Lop Nor nuclear test site. Most of the U-2 missions, however, were

Sometimes the slipper tanks on the U-2C were faired into the wing with small leading edge extensions. Other times they were not. No reason, or pattern, has been found to explain this. The location of the main and rear landing gear wells are illustrated. The insides of the wheel wells are painted gloss white to allow crews to detect hydraulic leaks. (Mick Roth)

Later in their lives, the Air Force U-2s dropped their national markings, even when operating within the United states. The BLACK VELVET paint proved to be fairly effective at visually hiding the aircraft at altitude, and the only markings generally carried were small red serial numbers on the vertical stabilizer. Reports that the serial numbers were randomly changed are most probably false. Like many early single-engine jets, the entire aft fuselage was removable to provide engine access. The maintenance personnel periodically did not reassemble the same aft fuselage to the same forward fuselage. Since the forward fuselage carried the aircraft's data plate (describing the serial number), the maintenance crews simply repainted the tail to match whatever aircraft it was attached to. (Lockheed Martin)

conducted around the periphery of denied territory using oblique angles at ranges approaching 100 miles. Intelligence flights were not confined to the Soviet Union. Egypt, Syria, Iraq, Saudi Arabia, Lebanon, and Yemen were all targets for the U-2, and on 6 December 1958 overflights began over the Chekiang and Kaingsi provinces of China – a location that would be visited frequently in the future.

Although each mission was carefully planned, U-2 pilots were, at least in the early years, given some amount of freedom to seek targets of opportunity. On one such occasion a U-2 pilot could not find the target he had been assigned in the

location expected, so he elected to follow a railroad spur 15 miles. At the end of the spur was what is now called Baikonur Cosmodrome, although at the time it was named Tyuratam by the CIA.

When the Air Force began receiving U-2s, they were assigned to the 4028th Strategic Reconnaissance Squadron (SRS) of the 4080th Strategic Reconnaissance Wing (SRW) at Laughlin AFB, Texas. The first U-2A arrived on 11 June 1957, over a year after the CIA began operating the type. By September the squadron had 15 U-2As and 5 WU-2As, along with approximately 40 pilots.

One of the first missions assigned to the Air Force U-2s was a High Altitude Sampling Program (HASP) sponsored by the Defense Atomic Support Agency. During OPERATION CROW FLIGHT the 4028th sampled over 150 million cubic feet of stratospheric air during a five year period using 45,000 flight hours. Typical missions were 7.5 hours long at cruising altitudes between 50,000 and 70,000 feet. Flights were conducted from a variety of locations, including: Puerto Rico; Buenos Aires; Alaska; North Dakota; and Australia. In addition to particulates and gases, the WU-2As gathered information on cosmic radiation, ozone accumulation, and upper atmospheric jet streams.

Article 347 (56-6680) in the two-tone grey camouflage that was used in the final few years in England. During most of this time the U-2Cs were configured with the Advanced Location Strike System (ALSS) configured in the Q-bay. The unusual tail markings were carried on all two-tone grey aircraft. This aircraft is currently on exhibit in the Smithsonian National Air and Space Museum. (Mick Roth Collection)

Much of the non-nuclear information came from sensors provided by NACA/NASA, and the data was in most cases shared with them.

When the Air Force was forced to retire the RB-57s acquired under project BALD EAGLE due to early wing fatigue, the U-2 was called in to take over surveillance programs such as TOY SOLDIER, GREEN HORNET, and SKY SHIELD. Quickly the U-2 became the primary strategic intelligence asset for the Air Force.

But the threat to the U-2 was growing. Although the fixed-site SA-1 system did not seem to represent a threat, but the newer semi-mobile SA-2 with a large booster motor and improved aerodynamics could potentially catch the U-2. Defensive electronics were finally fitted to the CIA U-2s during 1958 in the form of System 9, a crude radar lock-breaker provided by Granger Associates that replaced the drag chute. Even so, it was obvious that the U-2's days as an overflight vehicle were numbered.

Before U-2 flights over the Soviet Union ended, however, there would be one flight that caused considerable embarrassment for the CIA and United States. On 1 May 1960, Francis Gary Powers, a veteran of 27 CIA U-2 missions, was assigned to photograph two major ICBM test locations at Sverdlovsk and Plesetck. Coincidentally, these were also the locations of some of the heaviest air defenses in the world. The U-2 (Article 360) on this flight was considered a "hanger queen" that had been plagued with a series of small, but seemingly unsolvable, problems. Most important of these was an engine that was extremely sensitive to compressor stalls and flame-outs at high altitudes.

Powers' mission was routine until he began his photo run 67,000 feet over Sverdlovsk. Powers reported feeling a dull explosion underneath and behind the aircraft and watching the sky turn a bright orange. The U-2's right wing dropped, but when Powers' corrected he found that the nose began to pitch downward. Later analysis by Kelly Johnson indicated the horizontal stabilizers had probably been badly damaged. Moments later, the main wing structure failed and both wings separated from the fuselage. The physical damage to the aircraft pinned Powers' legs under the

Although the U-2 program had survived for 17 years without a two-seat trainer, continuing losses of aircraft and pilots, particularly during landing, forced the Air Force to procure two U-2C(T) trainers. Each of these was converted from an existing single-seat aircraft, and both spent their years in a glossy all white paint scheme. These two aircraft would also serve the first ten years of the U-2R program until dedicated two-seaters were built in the last production batch. (Michael Grove via the Mick Roth Collection)

instrument panel, eliminating any possibility of ejecting. Instead, Powers' elected to leave the aircraft by manually opening the canopy, and eventually separating from the remaining pieces of the aircraft at 15,000 feet before parachuting successfully to the ground.

In 1965 Soviet Colonel Oleg Penkovsky wrote a book that indicated the Soviets had fired a salvo of 14 SA-2s, and that it was the concussion from the detonating warheads that had brought down the U-2. Soviet examination of the wreckage indicated that none of the missiles or shrapnel had actually impacted the aircraft, although a Sukhoi Su-9 interceptor was inadvertently claimed by one of the SA-2s.

It was the U-2's most visible moment. The Soviets put Powers on trial, gaining a great deal of sympathy from the Third World in the process. Powers would be released two years later, but the damage was done. U-2 overflights of Soviet territory ceased. Since the U-2s were providing approximately 90% of the hard photographic data on the Soviet Union, this severely hampered U.S. intelligence operations. Powers himself was hired by Kelly Johnson as a test pilot, a position he held until his retirement in 1976. A year later he was killed while flying a television traffic helicopter in Los Angeles.

The bulging Q-bay of the two-tone grey aircraft held 18 Advanced Location Strike System (ALSS) sensors, nine per side. To flight-test the new system, the remaining seven Air Force U-2C aircraft were equipped with ALSS equipment in 1972. The system encountered serious development problems and it was not until 1975 that an operational test with five U-2Cs was finally conducted in Europe as Exercise CONSTANT TREAT. (Chris Pocock via the Mick Roth Collection)

Although hardly the end of U-2 operations, the Powers incident did have a profound effect, and the remaining CIA detachments in Turkey and Japan were recalled to the United States. At the same time, however, the Air Force U-2s were beginning to be operated more in the public eye, including inviting the press to a deployment of three aircraft to RAF Upper Heyford. During 1962 the Air Force took on increased responsibility for U-2 operations. Partly this was due to the embarrassment from the Pow-

ers' incident, and partly from the CIA's interest in their U-2 replacement, the Lockheed A-12 Blackbird, which was entering flight test.

However, before the CIA withdrew completely, one mission would be flown that brought the world to the brink of war. It was a CIA U-2 overflight of Cuba that first detected the installation of Soviet intermediate-range ballistic missiles. The CIA had been conducting two overflights of the island per month as part of their routine surveillance program. After

Captain Robert Rendleman and Article 367 (56-6700) had a bad day on 29 May 1975 when the aircraft was written off near Winterberg, West Germany. Rendleman ejected safely. The loss was well reported in the world press. The Air Force was down to six operational U-2Cs. (U.S. Air Force)

At least five small wing U-2s were lost over the Chinese mainland, including the four shown here on display outside the Beijing People's Museum. Each of the aircraft is remarkably intact for having been shot down from high altitude, and are undeniably U-2s. (Central Intelligence Agency)

detecting the missiles, this was increased to once per week. The CIA was either unable or unwilling to increase the frequency further, and the Air Force took this opportunity to lobby President Kennedy to take over the Cuban operations.

On 9 October 1962 the Air Force received the President's permission. Two Air Force pilots from the 4028th SRS were assigned the mission but, interestingly, they used CIA aircraft since Air Force U-2s still lacked electronic countermeasure

Another Dragon Lady outside the Beijing People's Museum. The larger air intakes identifies this as a U-2C, and it apparently was equipped with slipper tanks when it was downed. The Chinese did not go to any great lengths to reassemble the aircraft, simply placing the pieces in close enough proximity to make sure everybody could identify it as an "American" U-2. (Central Intelligence Agency)

systems. This was the beginning of the end for CIA U-2 operations in most of the world.

The first Air Force overflight of Cuba came back with startling results. Major Steve Heyser took off on 14 October and verified that the Soviets had placed missiles in Cuba. Why this should have been such a surprise is not clear since the United States had already deployed Jupiter IRBMs within range of Moscow in Italy and Turkey. This discovery caused a marked increase in U-2 overflights of Cuba. Missions were launched from Laughlin AFB, Texas, McCoy AFB (now Orlando International), Florida, or Barksdale AFB, Louisiana, several times per day. Between 14 October and 6 December, a total of 102 Air Force U-2 missions were flown.

On 27 October, Major Rudolph Anderson was shot down by an SA-2 over the Cuban naval base at Banes. It was the only U-2 loss to enemy fire over Cuba, although two other pilots would lose their lives to non-combat causes during overflights. The next day, the Soviets agreed to withdraw the missiles from Cuba, effectively ending the crisis.

A little-known exception to ending CIA involvement was an operation in Nationalist China where the CIA had conceived the idea of using the "free Chinese" in an overhead reconnaissance effort during 1958. After a lengthy instruction program at Laughlin AFB, three Martin RB-57Ds were turned over to the Taiwanese at Tao Yuan AB. These aircraft were followed by five U-2As that, on paper at least, Lockheed had "sold" to Taiwan. In reality, these aircraft were operated by the CIA, although usually with Republic of

China Air Force (RoCAF) pilots. Thirty RoCAF pilots were sent to U.S. to receive flight training in the U-2, and twenty-seven completed their training. On 14 December 1960, "Det H" was created on Taiwan, and would remain under CIA control until the end of 1974.

Meanwhile, despite the loss of at least a dozen aircraft and ten pilots, the Air Force still had 20 U-2s on strength in 1963. HASP missions were still the most frequently flown, but there were also numerous classified surveillance missions of various nations, excluding the Soviet Union and China. The HASP missions were finally terminated in March 1964 when the nuclear test ban treaty became effective and no further atmospheric tests were conducted (except one by South Africa in the 1970s). It was probably just as well, since three months earlier President Johnson had committed the U-2s to reconnaissance missions over Vietnam.

The Air Force U-2s were reconfigured to carry larger ELINT payloads and deployed to Bien Hoa AB near Saigon under OPERATION DRAGON LADY. The first sortie was flown in January 1964, and the flights would continue for nearly 12 years

This HASP U-2A has the "hard nose" sampling unit in addition to the one located on the far side of the Q-bay. A door in the front of the hard nose opened, allowing particulates to be captured in canisters and on paper filters inside. The glass dome for the sextant can be seen immediately in front of the canopy. A variety of antennas and air data tubes protrude from the nose. (Lockheed Martin)

from various bases in Vietnam, Laos, and Thailand. The increased effectiveness of North Vietnam's air defenses eventually caused the U-2s to be moved to a stand-off surveillance mode, and overflight missions were increasingly conducted by RF-4Cs and unmanned remotely piloted vehicles (RPV – drones). Though the U-2 had been under continual improvement, especially the incorporation of improved ECM equipment, it was nonetheless beginning to show its age. The Air Force was also running out of them.

The two-seat U-2D models had a second cockpit in the Q-bay. This photo gives a good reference for the size of the MIDAS infrared sensor installed in the turret between the two cockpits. The fairing on top of the aft canopy is to smooth the slipstream behind the MIDAS sensor. The rear cockpit was intended as a research station and had basic flight instrumentation, but no flight controls. Both cockpits had ejection seats. (U.S. Air Force via the Tony Landis Collection)

BIG WING DRAGON LADIES

Although the U-2C was still providing valuable intelligence, the continued incorporation of more and heavier sensors and ECM equipment was rapidly taking its toll on performance. Late in its life, the U-2C had less than half the range of the original U-2As, and its maximum altitude had decreased by almost 5,000 feet. Additionally, over 40 of the original 55 airframes had been lost to various causes, including at least five shot down over China, one over Cuba, and several over and around the Soviet Union.

Over the years Kelly Johnson had been tinkering with advanced U-2 versions, beginning with a modified U-2C sometimes referred to as the U-2L ("L" probably stool for "long" or "lengthened" instead of being an official designation). This aircraft stretched the basic U-2 airframe by five feet using a 30-inch plug ahead and behind the wing, and increased the wingspan eight feet. Johnson even evaluated using the U-2L to carry a 240-inch focal length camera that pointed upward to photograph orbiting Soviet satellites. In September 1963 Johnson proposed building 25 U-2Ls for the Air Force at a cost of $1.1 million each.

Two further years of refinement resulted in the Model CL-351, and in August 1966 Lockheed was awarded a contract to begin development of the new aircraft. The major goals of the new model were to provide greater payload capacity, and to restore the range and altitude capabilities of the original U-2. Better cruise stability and landing characteristics were also highly desired. The model was referred to as U-2R, with the "R" meaning "redesigned" or "revised;" however the designation later became official.

To the pilots, the most welcome change was a larger cockpit. The original U-2's cockpit had been so small, especially after the incorporation of an ejection seat, that only a partial pressure suit could be worn. The U-2R pilots would enjoy the luxury of a full pressure suit (initially the A/P-22S-2). The U-2R would also be equipped with a zero-zero ejection seat capable of meaningful escape throughout the aircraft's operating range. Although the driftsight was retained since it had proved exceptionally useful in providing a means for the pilot to determine the tactical situation beneath him, the sextant was discarded since Inertial Navigation Systems (INS) were now sufficiently accurate and reliable.

The U-2R was almost 40 percent larger than the original U-2, with a 23-foot increase in wingspan. Total wing area increased by 400 square feet, but the wing structural weight was reduced by 3 pounds per square foot. Interestingly, six feet of the outer wing panels of all the new aircraft were hinged to allow folding for storage, partially because it was expected the U-2R would operate from aircraft carriers, as did its predecessors, and partially to allow storage in standard Air Force hangers. Hydraulically actuated outboard (roll) and inboard (lift dumping) spoilers were added to

A U-2C and a U-2R pose on the ramp at North Base. Interestingly, by this time the U-2C had received a black sun shade, while the newer U-2R uses a white one. The two aircraft are really completely different, sharing little more than the basic configuration. (Lockheed Martin Skunk Works via Denny Lombard)

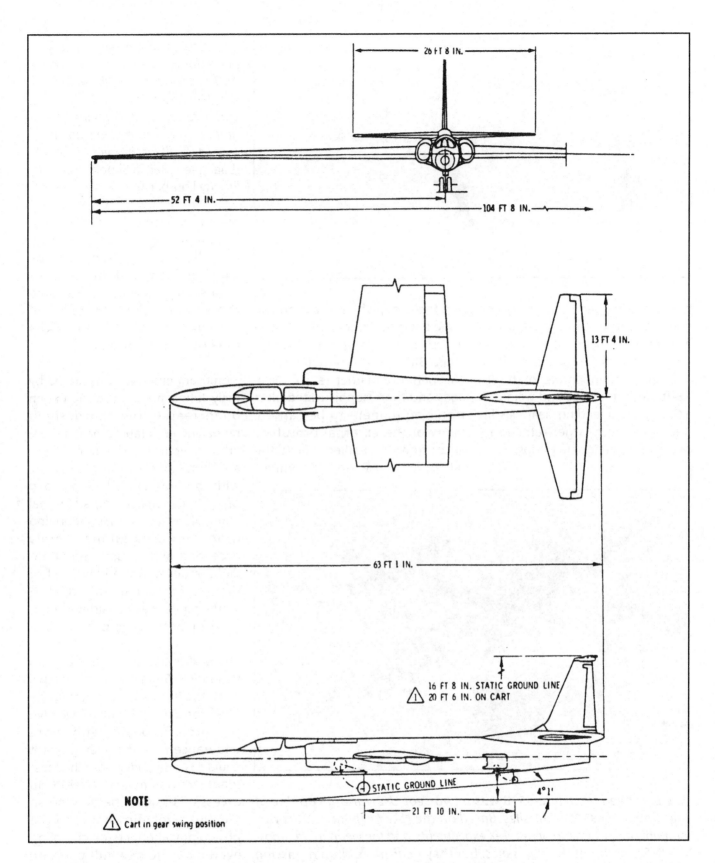

The U-2R is a large aircraft, with a wing span of 104 feet, 8 inches, and an overall length of 63 feet 1 inch. The outer six feet of the wings fold upward to assist in ground handling and hanger storage. Surprisingly, the entire aircraft can be disassembled and carried by a single C-141 transport when it needs to deploy overseas. Several other C-141 worth of supplies and maintenance tools are also required to support deployment. (U.S. Air Force)

A U-2R takes off, leaving behind its pogos for the ground crew to pick up. The pogo solution allowed a simpler and lighter airframe, but added certain complications on the ground, as well as making landing more difficult for the pilot. (Lockheed Martin Skunk Works via Denny Lombard)

the top mid-span surface of each wing ahead of the conventional trailing edge flaps. The horizontal and vertical stabilizers were enlarged to compensate for the aircraft's increased size and weight. A strengthened landing gear was fitted along with larger retractable wing leading edge stall strips.

The fuselage, while retaining the same basic configuration as its predecessor, was totally new and provided 30% more internal volume. This permitted larger sensor packages and more sophisticated electronic equipment to be carried. Many of the external protuberances from the earlier aircraft, the oil cooler and various antennas, were built into the airframe from the beginning. The new fuselage also dictated a longer tailpipe which helped mask the engine's infrared signature, and eliminated the need for the "sugar scoop" masking device used under the exhaust of earlier aircraft.

Significant emphasis was placed by Kelly Johnson and his design team on increasing the new design's range and endurance. The first-generation aircraft had suffered from an inherent fuel capacity limitation; with their maximum internal load of 1,345 gallons and an additional 200 gallons in external underwing drop tanks, endurance rarely exceeded nine hours. Though in-flight refueling was added to a few first-generation aircraft, the aircraft's range was considered marginal for many missions.

The U-2R made up for this by providing 2,915 gallons in its integral wing tanks, totally eliminating the need for external tanks. This gave the aircraft considerably more endurance than the average pilot could tolerate under even the most ideal circumstances. Missions in excess of 14 hours became possible, but rarely flown due to the physiological effects on the pilot, even with the new full pressure suits. Since the built-in range was more than sufficient, none of the U-2Rs would be equipped for in-flight refueling. The U-2R has a ferry

The Lockheed Model CL-351B was a two-seat U-2 variant capable of carrying at least four missiles. Based on the NAVY markings, this was probably an outgrowth of the EP-X experiments, and the weapons are most likely Penguin anti-ship missiles, but they bear more than a passing resemblance to AIM-54 Phoenix air-to-air missiles. Most armed U-2 proposals, including this one, used a more conventional tricycle landing gear with the main gear housed in the small pods at mid-wing. (Lockheed Martin Skunk Works via Denny Lombard)

The U-2R introduced a larger cockpit that finally allowed the pilots to use a full pressure suit instead of the partial pressure suit used in small wing U-2s. This is a S1031 pressure suit and its associated ground air conditioning pack. The scoop located on top of the U-2R's nose leads to a heat exchanger for the ASARS-2 components inside the flat-sided nose section. (Lockheed Martin Skunk Works via Denny Lombard)

range of just over 8,000 miles, almost 3,000 miles greater than the U-2C and essentially the same as the original U-2A.

The non-afterburning 17,000 lbf Pratt & Whitney J75-P-13B used in later U-2Cs was selected for use in the U-2R since it was sufficiently powerful and had a good reliability record. Additionally, Pratt & Whitney continuously upgraded and tweaked the specialized J75-P-13 series' design and had promised Lockheed improved cruise thrust and economy at altitude.

Since the original U-2s were carrier capable, it was decided from the beginning that the U-2R would be able to operate off of the large-deck carriers. Therefore one U-2R was taken to the USS America (CVA-66) for trials during November 1969. Lockheed test pilot Bill Park flew the initial qualification flights, and several other pilots were checked out subsequently. A small quantity of carrier modification kits were produced for the U-2R, but as far as is known, no operational missions have ever been flown. The protective guard on the wingtip shows up well here, installed to ensure the wing-tip skid plate did not get tangled in the arresting wires. (Lockheed Martin Skunk Works via Denny Lombard)

The Q-bay concept of the original U-2 had proven extremely versatile, and was retained for the U-2R. In fact, the concept was expanded by providing an interchangeable nose section, as well as structural provisions for large "superpods" at midspan that could house sensors and other equipment. The pods were not initially used by the U-2R, but would later prove invaluable. All of the aircraft's equipment was kept separated from the sensor payloads, greatly easing the job of reconfiguring the aircraft to carry different sensors. At least this was the idea. Unfortunately, many of the sensors the U-2R would end up carrying had not even been conceived when the aircraft was designed, and by the 1990s most airframes were dedicated to specific sensors or small combinations of sensors, greatly reducing their flexibility.

Although Lockheed had anticipated a large production contract for the new U-2, budget and political considerations resulted in only 12 aircraft being ordered in September 1966. Of these, six were for the CIA and six for the Air Force, which codenamed them SENIOR YEAR. A full-scale mock-up was reviewed in late November 1966, and the only major change was the stated preference by the Air Force to retain

There are remarkably few photographs available of the Republic of China U-2 operations. The six pilots pictured represent the last class to go through flight training prior to the CIA withdrawing the U-2Rs from service. Unlike U.S. U-2R operations that were flown with no national insignia, a small ROC insignia is located immediately above the speed brakes. Noteworthy are the folded wingtips in the head-on shot. (Clarence J. P. Fu Collection)

The first U-2R (Article 051) was first flown without paint using the civilian registration number N803X. Lockheed test pilot Bill Park made the flight on 28 August 1967 from the CIA facility on North Base. The trailing edge flaps did not yet contain the cut-out for the superpods, and a long probe with alpha and beta vanes was fitted to the nose to perform calibrations of the flight instruments. (Lockheed Martin Skunk Works via the Tony Landis Collection)

the "old fashioned" round instrumentation used in the U-2C instead of the newer "tape" instruments preferred by Lockheed. As it turned out, only the first U-2R (Article 051) used the new-style instruments, with production machines reverting back to the more familiar dials. Unlike the original U-2 production, the U-2R would be manufactured at the Lockheed plant in Burbank.

Lockheed test pilot Bill Park made the first flight using N803X (Article 051) on 28 August 1967 from the CIA facility at North Base on the edge of Edwards AFB. A few minor problems emerged during the flight test program, including a slower than expected roll rate, solved by adding a second pair of hydraulically-actuated spoilers outboard on the wing. The new wing could flex as much as four feet at the tip, disconcerting until you expected it. Above 60,000 feet the aircraft demonstrated marginal stability in all axes and required a stability augmentation system and reliable autopilot.

The second U-2R arrived at North Base in February 1968 and training of both CIA and Air Force pilots commenced. By December 1968, all 12 aircraft had been delivered.

The production tooling was removed from Burbank during 1969 and placed in storage at Norton AFB, California. The CIA's six U-2Rs were assigned to North Base, while all six of the Air Force's SENIOR YEAR aircraft were based at Davis-Monthan AFB, Arizona. The Air Force began to deploy their aircraft during the fall of 1968 by sending U-2Rs to an "operating location" at McCoy AFB (OL-19) and Bien Hoa, Vietnam (OL-20).

Two U-2Rs were delivered to the Det H in Taiwan following a non-stop delivery flight from Edwards AFB. These aircraft represented fully one third of the entire CIA U-2R fleet, demonstrating the Agency's commitment to surveillance of mainland China. The first U-2R loss occurred in November 1968 when a Chinese pilot lost control during a cross-wind landing at Tao Yuan. Both CIA and Nationalist Chinese pilots conducted overflight missions until October 1974, when the

The main fuselage for a U-2R (or, more probably, a TR-1) is lifted into position for final assembly. The aft fuselage, like that on the original U-2, is separate and is removed to access the engine. The nose section is also modular to accommodate different sensor packages. The wings and horizontal stabilizer can be removed to allow a disassembled U-2R to fit inside a single C-141 for transport to remote sites. (Lockheed Martin)

The U.S. Navy borrowed two U-2Rs from the CIA to investigate their use as an experimental electronics platform (EP-X). One of the U-2Rs (Article 060) was finished in mostly natural metal, with a light grey paint being applied to the bottom of the fuselage to protect it against sea water splashing. The other U-2R (Article 061) was painted the standard BLACK VELVET. Both had Navy markings on the fuselage and wings. Although the EP-X project proved the viability of using a high-altitude long-endurance platform for sea surveillance, advances in satellite technology overtook the concept and no Navy U-2s were ever built. (Lockheed Martin)

Nixon accords led to a cessation of all overflights of mainland China.

Since this was the last major U-2 operation being conducted by the CIA, all Agency U-2 assets were turned over to the Air Force within the next year. This, however, caused an interesting problem. The CIA had very purposefully <u>not</u> identified any of their equipment with markings, notices, instructions, etc., in an effort to hide its origin if it should fall into enemy hands (allowing the United States to deny it was a U.S. aircraft). But the military logistics system was highly dependent upon items being clearly marked and identified, and a great deal of effort was required to sort through the CIA material and bring it up to Air Force marking standards.

During November 1969 Lockheed test pilot Bill Park demonstrated the U-2R's carrier suitability aboard the USS America (CVA-66) off the coast of Virginia. This was also a demonstration of Park's abilities since he had gained his flight experience as an Air Force fighter pilot and was totally unaccustomed to the concept of carrier operations. Both the U-2 and Park survived intact.

A 45° flap setting and an approach speed of 72 knots with 20 knots wind-over-the-deck was selected for the demonstrations and since the U-2R does not have an angle of attack indicator, the approaches were flown relying solely on indicated airspeed and "feel." However, when the day finally came to demonstrate the carrier landing capability to Navy and CIA officials, Park ran into a minor problem. As he started his final approach to the America, indications were that the tail hook had not deployed. Park waved-off the approach and returned to shore where it was discovered that the locking pin had not been removed from the newly installed tailhook.

A quick turnaround soon had the U-2 over the ship again and Park

The U-2R did not have any particular problems qualifying aboard the USS America (CVA-66). Take offs were accomplished without the catapult, using runs of under 300 feet with 20 knots over the deck. The U-2 proved it could reliably snag an arresting wire, although aligning the centerline was a little more critical than usual because of the aircraft's long wingspan. The outer six feet of the wings folded, allowing the U-2R to fit aboard the elevators and into the hanger deck. No operational U-2R missions were ever flown from a carrier deck, although several modification kits were built as a contingency. (Lockheed Martin)

demonstrated a rather anticlimactic series of landings, with deck runs averaging 300 feet. After one landing, the U-2's wings were folded and the aircraft lowered to the hanger deck to demonstrate its deck handling characteristics The Navy, CIA, and Lockheed were satisfied with the results and the aircraft officially became carrier capable. Accordingly, Lockheed was awarded a small contract to produce a field modification kit consisting of the arresting hook and associated fairings, rear landing gear cable deflectors, wing tip skid extensions, and wing tip skid cable deflectors. Additionally, a switch and indicator was added to the right console panel on all subsequent production U-2Rs to control the arresting hook. Unlike the original U-2s, however, the U-2R was never used operationally off a carrier.

Expanding on these tests during early 1973, the Navy began to evaluate the U-2R as an experimental electronics patrol (EP-X) platform and borrowed two CIA U-2Rs to test the viability of the concept. The modified aircraft were delivered to North Base during early 1973, and the program ran until the end of the year with the majority of the test missions being flown off the southern California coast. The Navy effort was intended to verify the effectiveness of the RCA-developed X-band radar mounted in an enlarged nose. A United Technologies AN/ALQ-110 electronic intelligence receiver was mounted in the right superpod, and an RCA Return Beam Vidicon (RBV) camera in the left superpod. All three were designed for real-time monitoring of maritime movements from high altitudes, and their data was downlinked via equipment located in the E-bay.

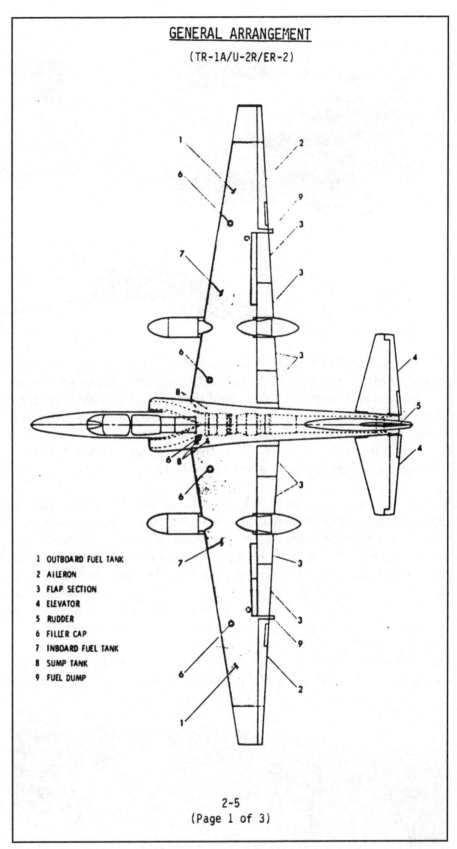

GENERAL ARRANGEMENT
(TR-1A/U-2R/ER-2)

1 OUTBOARD FUEL TANK
2 AILERON
3 FLAP SECTION
4 ELEVATOR
5 RUDDER
6 FILLER CAP
7 INBOARD FUEL TANK
8 SUMP TANK
9 FUEL DUMP

2-5
(Page 1 of 3)

The overall configuration of the U-2R is extremely conventional. Not noted on the legend here are the two superpods (mid span on each wing), and the folding wingtips (shown by a line inboard from the tip). (U.S. Air Force)

The first five U-2Rs are seen at the CIA facility at North Base. The first prototype (Article 051) is in the foreground. All five aircraft have white heat shields on their canopies. As built, all of the first 12 U-2Rs were identical except for the cockpit instrumentation in Article 051. Shortly after they began operations, it was discovered that the horizontal stabilizers were suffering from a mild buffet, and external stiffeners were added, giving the stabilizers a "ribbed" appearance. (Lockheed Martin)

Later, the X-band radar was removed from the Q-bay of one aircraft and replaced by a Texas Instruments AN/APS-116, a purpose-built sea surveillance system designed for the Lockheed S-3 Viking anti-submarine aircraft. To provide 360° coverage, Lockheed developed a unique inflatable Kevlar radome that covered the antenna when it was lowered from the Q-bay. Maintenance access to the antenna was provided by a zipper, taken from a U-2's partial pressure suit, sewn into the Kevlar radome. The advent of advanced satellite systems capable of providing constant wide ocean surveillance led to the Navy losing interest in the EP-X concept. Nevertheless, the results of these trials were used by Lockheed to generate a proposal using the U-2R in the sea control role. This armed U-2 carried six Rockwell Condor anti-ship missiles under the wings, but unfortunately, the Navy expressed little interest. The inflatable radome would find further use during the Air Force SENIOR LANCE side-looking radar tests.

In July 1970 the Air Force contracted Lockheed to integrate an E-Systems/Melpar COMINT sensor and datalink developed as part of project SENIOR SPEAR into the U-2R. The COMINT system was carried by one of the latest drone variants, but typical of Skunk Works, Lockheed improved upon the system with better antennas and a new Sperry datalink. The antennas and some of the electronics were carried in small pods mounted at mid-span on each wing.

The SENIOR SPEAR systems were operated by the Air Force as part of operation SENIOR BOOK. From race-track orbits over the Gulf of Tonkin, the SENIOR SPEAR U-2s eavesdropped on Vietnamese communications, transmitting the data in real-time to a ground station at Nakhon Phanom on the Thai border. SENIOR BOOK missions continued until April 1976, although at least two U-2Rs were lost in combat during the Vietnam War.

The wings of all U-2Rs fold to enable them to fit aboard aircraft carriers, and also into most Air Force hangers. The folding mechanism is completely manual, and three bolts must be removed from each wing. The interleaving fixtures provide a load path to the spars, and also serve as the location for the bolts. A small removable strip on the upper wing surface covers the bolt access. (Lockheed Martin)

The Pratt & Whitney J75-P-13 engine was used in the U-2C and all big wing U-2s except for the U-2S. The engine was a modification of the basic engine used in the F-105 and F-106 fighters, and it was largely the retirement of the last of these that caused Lockheed to seek a new powerplant for the U-2S. Almost all the engine accessories are mounted in a package below the engine's high-pressure compressor section. (Pratt & Whitney)

A little known experiment was conducted in the 1970s when a U-2R was equipped with a trapeze launcher under each wing using the support structure intended for the superpods. Each trapeze carried a small Beechcraft drone that was supposed to be used as a SAM decoy during overflights. This concept was briefly flight tested, including at least one launch, before it was cancelled and the U-2R was relegated to using more traditional ECM systems.

But the U-2R, like the small-wing versions that preceded it, was best deployed as a camera platform. Thanks mainly to better and faster computer modeling techniques, the original Type-B camera had been improved by Hycon with better optics and lighter construction. The new camera was designated HR-73B and had first been used on late U-2C missions. A newer Type-H (HR-329) camera is the most widely used on the U-2R. Manufactured by Hycon based on the Type IV camera developed for the A-12, this unit is also known as the Long-Range Oblique Photographic (LOROP) camera, and is used at oblique angles from a position well outside enemy territory. The Type-H camera uses a high resolution, gyro-stabilized framing system with a 66-inch focal length lens with a folded optical path. The camera was first introduced on the U-2C during 1965.

Traditionally, the Type-H camera operates at an slant angle to provide greater coverage, however during DESERT STORM, planners experimented with the camera aimed straight down at the nadir position. The detail and clarity impressed planners and amazed theater commanders. Commanders were disappointed, however, that the system could not provide the same detail and clarity at greater ranges, and that technicians had to process the film after the aircraft landed.

The early U-2s had frequently been used as surrogates to test cameras for the CORONA spy satellites, and in an odd turn of events, panoramic camera systems developed by Itek for later spy satellites were adapted for airborne use as the Intelligence Reconnaissance Imaging System (IRIS). These 24- and 36-inch focal length cameras were mounted on an Optical Bar Assembly and were used by both the U-2R and SR-71. They could scan a 140° swath beneath the aircraft, translating to a width of approximately 35 miles at 70,000 feet. At least three variations (IRIS-I, -II, and -III) were produced. The IRIS-III provides wider "synoptic" coverage than the Type-H camera, but it does not have the resolution quality.

IMAGES FROM LARGE DRAGONS

THE U-2R BECOMES OPERATIONAL

When it received its first U-2R in late 1968, the 100th SRW was primarily responsible for continuing reconnaissance of Cuba, and a single U-2R was deployed to OL-19 at Barksdale AFB. In August 1970 an overflight detected new construction at the port of Cicnfugos, which led to an international debate over whether the Soviet Union was about to base ballistic missile submarines in Cuba. The U-2 flights were stepped up, and the Dragon Lady again found itself challenged by Cuban MiGs. The Soviet Union later decided not to deploy the submarines to Cuba, and no U-2Rs were lost over Cuba.

During August 1970, two CIA U-2Rs were sent to monitor an uneasy cease fire in the Middle East. Flights were flown from RAF Akrotiri, Cyprus, two or three times per week, but were suspended in early November after Egypt objected.

The aircraft returned to the United States later in November. Three years later, following the October 1973 Yom Kippur war, the operation was resumed with the approval of both Israel and Egypt. The war's aftermath had resulted in a buffer zone and the U-2s were used to ensure no unauthorized intrusions were made. The Cyprus operation was known as "Det G" and employed both American and British pilots. Later, airborne reconnaissance of the Sinai and the Golan Heights was formalized in the Camp David peace agreements,

When the initial batch of U-2Rs transited through various bases they generally wore a simple star-and-bar insignia on their intake. The insignia was usually removed prior to flying operational missions. Article 054 (68-10332) was initially assigned to the CIA. Note the black sun shade on top of the canopy. Both a whip antenna and a blade antenna have been installed on top of the fuselage above the national insignia. (Lockheed Martin)

Engine testing on the U-2R. Rather unusually, it appears the forward fuselage has been removed, leaving only the wings (containing the fuel) and engine. Notice the man with the control stick sitting on top of the block. (Tony Landis Collection)

AIRCRAFT MAJOR DRAWINGS
(TR-1A/U-2R/ER-2)

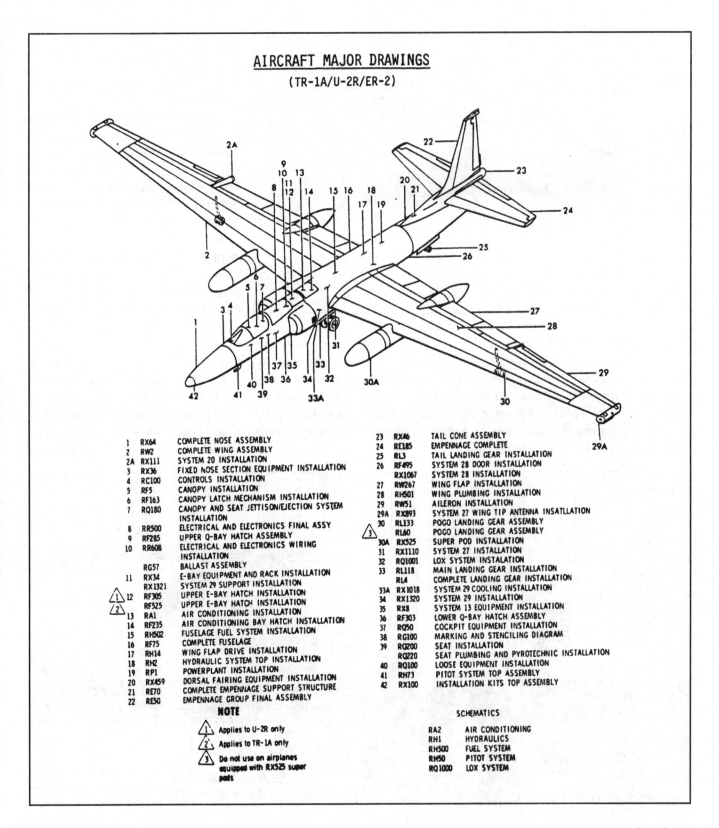

1	RX64	COMPLETE NOSE ASSEMBLY
2	RW2	COMPLETE WING ASSEMBLY
2A	RX111	SYSTEM 20 INSTALLATION
3	RX36	FIXED NOSE SECTION EQUIPMENT INSTALLATION
4	RC100	CONTROLS INSTALLATION
5	RF5	CANOPY INSTALLATION
6	RF163	CANOPY LATCH MECHANISM INSTALLATION
7	RQ180	CANOPY AND SEAT JETTISON/EJECTION SYSTEM INSTALLATION
8	RR500	ELECTRICAL AND ELECTRONICS FINAL ASSY
9	RF285	UPPER Q-BAY HATCH ASSEMBLY
10	RR608	ELECTRICAL AND ELECTRONICS WIRING INSTALLATION
	RG57	BALLAST ASSEMBLY
11	RX34	E-BAY EQUIPMENT AND RACK INSTALLATION
	RX1321	SYSTEM 29 SUPPORT INSTALLATION
12	RF305	UPPER E-BAY HATCH INSTALLATION
	RF525	UPPER E-BAY HATCH INSTALLATION
13	RA1	AIR CONDITIONING INSTALLATION
14	RF235	AIR CONDITIONING BAY HATCH INSTALLATION
15	RH502	FUSELAGE FUEL SYSTEM INSTALLATION
16	RF75	COMPLETE FUSELAGE
17	RH14	WING FLAP DRIVE INSTALLATION
18	RH2	HYDRAULIC SYSTEM TOP INSTALLATION
19	RP1	POWERPLANT INSTALLATION
20	RX459	DORSAL FAIRING EQUIPMENT INSTALLATION
21	RE70	COMPLETE EMPENNAGE SUPPORT STRUCTURE
22	RE50	EMPENNAGE GROUP FINAL ASSEMBLY

23	RX46	TAIL CONE ASSEMBLY
24	RE185	EMPENNAGE COMPLETE
25	RL3	TAIL LANDING GEAR INSTALLATION
26	RF495	SYSTEM 28 DOOR INSTALLATION
	RX1067	SYSTEM 28 INSTALLATION
27	RW267	WING FLAP INSTALLATION
28	RH501	WING PLUMBING INSTALLATION
29	RW51	AILERON INSTALLATION
29A	RX893	SYSTEM 27 WING TIP ANTENNA INSATLLATION
30	RL133	POGO LANDING GEAR ASSEMBLY
	RL60	POGO LANDING GEAR ASSEMBLY
30A	RX525	SUPER POD INSTALLATION
31	RX1110	SYSTEM 27 INSTALLATION
32	RQ1001	LOX SYSTEM INSTALATION
33	RL118	MAIN LANDING GEAR INSTALLATION
	RL4	COMPLETE LANDING GEAR INSTALLATION
33A	RX1018	SYSTEM 29 COOLING INSTALLATION
34	RX1320	SYSTEM 29 INSTALLATION
35	RX8	SYSTEM 13 EQUIPMENT INSTALLATION
36	RF303	LOWER Q-BAY HATCH ASSEMBLY
37	RQ50	COCKPIT EQUIPMENT INSTALLATION
38	RG100	MARKING AND STENCILING DIAGRAM
39	RQ200	SEAT INSTALLATION
	RQ220	SEAT PLUMBING AND PYROTECHNIC INSTALLATION
40	RQ100	LOOSE EQUIPMENT INSTALLATION
41	RH73	PITOT SYSTEM TOP ASSEMBLY
42	RX100	INSTALLATION KITS TOP ASSEMBLY

NOTE

1. Applies to U-2R only
2. Applies to TR-1A only
3. Do not use on airplanes equipped with RX525 super pods

SCHEMATICS

RA2	AIR CONDITIONING
RH1	HYDRAULICS
RH500	FUEL SYSTEM
RH50	PITOT SYSTEM
RQ1000	LOX SYSTEM

It takes a lot of drawings to document a modern aircraft. There are 46 top-level drawings referenced on this chart, and each of those refers the user to an entire series of drawings, schematics, and parts lists. This was one of the major changes for the TR-1 program. The original U-2s, and the first batch of U-2Rs, had been developed largely in secret with the CIA as the primary customer, and documentation had been kept to a minimum. The Air Force was the only customer for the TR-1, and the program had to largely conform to normal military documentation requirements. (U.S. Air Force)

and the data from the U-2 flights was shared between all parties. When the CIA detachment at Akrotiri was disbanded at the end of 1974, it was taken over by the Air Force 100th SRW under the code-name OLIVE HARVEST.

The Dragon Lady was finally withdrawn from Thailand in April 1976. Three months earlier, the 100th SRW was equipped with U-2s and deployed to Osan AB, South Korea, where it had been operating various model drones. Despite their contributions to intelligence gathering during Vietnam, the unmanned vehicles soon fell out of favor as the U.S. defense budget fell, and the remaining drones and their DC-130 motherships were transferred to the Tactical Air Command (TAC). When the drones were transferred from SAC to TAC, the

Article 073 (80-1073) returns to Beale AFB from a training mission. The hangers in the background were specially built to house the fleet of SR-71 Blackbirds, and the U-2 hangers are behind and to the right of them. Small protrusions on the wing tips and the top of the vertical stabilizer contain antennas for the various defensive electronic systems. Notice the slightly nose-down approach angle – typical for tail-draggers but a new concept for jet fighter pilots. (Lockheed Martin)

It takes a while to hook up a pressure-suited pilot in the cockpit and get the U-2 ready for flight. The hot desert sun at Davis-Monthan convinced the Air Force that some manner of protection was required, giving birth to this canvas sunshade attached to the boarding stairs. The idea caught on and similar setups are used at most operating locations. (Lockheed Martin)

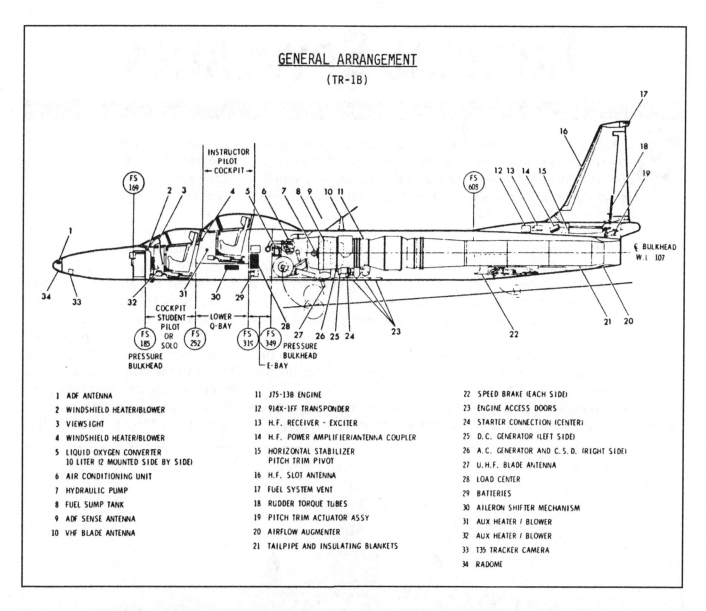

GENERAL ARRANGEMENT
(TR-1B)

1 ADF ANTENNA	11 J75-13B ENGINE	22 SPEED BRAKE (EACH SIDE)
2 WINDSHIELD HEATER/BLOWER	12 914X-1FF TRANSPONDER	23 ENGINE ACCESS DOORS
3 VIEWSIGHT	13 H.F. RECEIVER - EXCITER	24 STARTER CONNECTION (CENTER)
4 WINDSHIELD HEATER/BLOWER	14 H.F. POWER AMPLIFIER/ANTENNA COUPLER	25 D.C. GENERATOR (LEFT SIDE)
5 LIQUID OXYGEN CONVERTER 10 LITER (2 MOUNTED SIDE BY SIDE)	15 HORIZONTAL STABILIZER PITCH TRIM PIVOT	26 A.C. GENERATOR AND C.S.D. (RIGHT SIDE)
6 AIR CONDITIONING UNIT	16 H.F. SLOT ANTENNA	27 U.H.F. BLADE ANTENNA
7 HYDRAULIC PUMP	17 FUEL SYSTEM VENT	28 LOAD CENTER
8 FUEL SUMP TANK	18 RUDDER TORQUE TUBES	29 BATTERIES
9 ADF SENSE ANTENNA	19 PITCH TRIM ACTUATOR ASSY	30 AILERON SHIFTER MECHANISM
10 VHF BLADE ANTENNA	20 AIRFLOW AUGMENTER	31 AUX HEATER / BLOWER
	21 TAILPIPE AND INSULATING BLANKETS	32 AUX HEATER / BLOWER
		33 T35 TRACKER CAMERA
		34 RADOME

There are currently four two-seat U-2S(T) aircraft (one is technically still a U-2R(T), but will be re-engined in 1998), all similar to the TR-1B shown here. With the exception of the second cockpit installed in the Q-bay, with its associated controls and displays, the two-seat aircraft are similar to the single-seat U-2R/S. The second seat is not easily removable, and the aircraft are not considered operationally capable. (U.S. Air Force)

100th SRW was left with only half a mission, and SAC's U-2s were combined with the SR-71s at Beale AFB under the 9th SRW umbrella in July 1976. The 100th SRW and its squadron numbers were reassigned to KC-135 units already at Beale, and the relocated U-2 squadron became the 99th SRS of the 9th SRW.

As the Iranian hostage crises deepened during 1979, the U.S. began expanding its military presence in the Indian Ocean. A single U-2R from the 99th SRW was detached to Diego Garcia, a location used occasionally in the past to monitor locations in and around the Indian Ocean. This detachment remained on a semi-permanent basis until the mid-1980s.

During August 1976 U-2Rs from the 99th SRS began deploying to RAF Mildenhall with increasing regularity. A permanent "Det 4" was established in 1979 with a single U-2R, and later, two SR-71As. This U-2R was usually configured for ELINT and COMINT surveillance and frequently flew missions lasting in excess of eight hours along the borders of the various European Communist bloc countries and the Soviet Union. This detachment would exist until the 17th RW was formed at RAF Alconbury in 1983.

TACTICAL SPYPLANES

But Kelly Johnson still wanted to produce more than a dozen U-2Rs. In a near desperate attempt during 1974 to keep the U-2R production line open, he proposed a "U-2R RPV" to compete with the forthcoming COMPASS COPE remotely piloted vehicles. The Air Force had decided that unmanned vehicles were the wave of the future and was ready to commit large amounts of funding to procure advanced high-performance RPVs. Primarily because it was based on an aircraft that already was in production, Lockheed argued that the U-2R RPV could be built for substantially less money than either of its competitors, and that it could accomplish the proposed mission more effectively. Although four COMPASS COPE prototypes were built (two Boeing YQM-94As and two Teledyne Ryan YQM-98As), a combination of technical, economic, and political problems ended the program prematurely. The same combination of problems also spelled the end of the U-2R RPV, and no production contract was forthcoming.

Concurrently, another program was underway to develop a system capable of identifying enemy air defense radar and communications sites by homing in on their electromagnetic emissions. The Precision Location Strike System (PLSS) would a require high-flying platform similar to the U-2 or COMPASS COPE. The complicated and expensive effort to produce PLSS had begun in 1972 as the Advanced Location Strike System (ALSS) under the theory that a group of ELINT sensor-equipped aircraft orbiting at high altitude and connected via a real-time datalink with ground stations could quickly determine the position of threat emitters. This

The obligatory overhead shot that every U-2 book must have. The large superpods were anticipated from the early days of the program, but were not actually flown initially. When they were added, the trailing edge flaps had to be reconfigured, resulting in a slight decrease in total flap area. The positioning of the speedbrakes on the fuselage sides is reminiscent of early jet fighters, including the F-104 that served as the inspiration for the U-2 design. (Lockheed Martin Skunk Works via Denny Lombard)

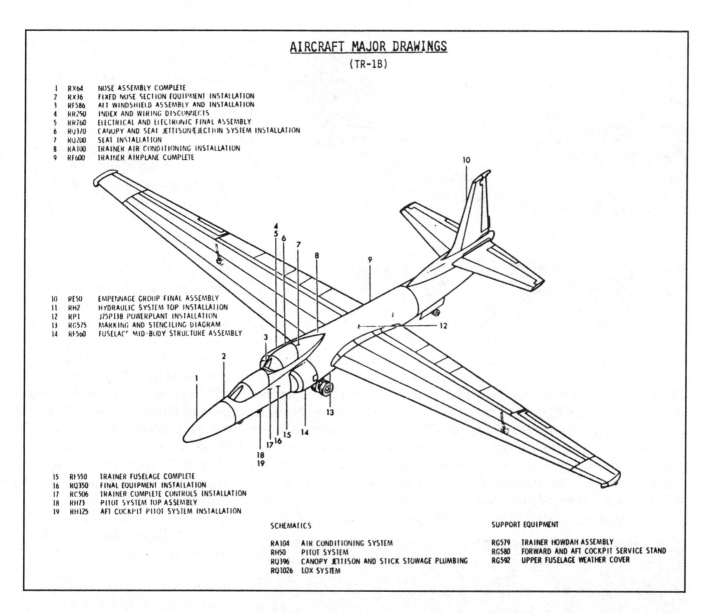

AIRCRAFT MAJOR DRAWINGS
(TR-1B)

1	RX64	NOSE ASSEMBLY COMPLETE
2	RX36	FIXED NOSE SECTION EQUIPMENT INSTALLATION
3	RF586	AFT WINDSHIELD ASSEMBLY AND INSTALLATION
4	RR250	INDEX AND WIRING DISCONNECTS
5	RR760	ELECTRICAL AND ELECTRONIC FINAL ASSEMBLY
6	RQ370	CANOPY AND SEAT JETTISON/EJECTION SYSTEM INSTALLATION
7	RQ200	SEAT INSTALLATION
8	RA100	TRAINER AIR CONDITIONING INSTALLATION
9	RF600	TRAINER AIRPLANE COMPLETE

10	RE50	EMPENNAGE GROUP FINAL ASSEMBLY
11	RH2	HYDRAULIC SYSTEM TOP INSTALLATION
12	RP1	J75P13B POWERPLANT INSTALLATION
13	RG575	MARKING AND STENCILING DIAGRAM
14	RF560	FUSELAGE MID-BODY STRUCTURE ASSEMBLY

15	RF550	TRAINER FUSELAGE COMPLETE
16	RQ350	FINAL EQUIPMENT INSTALLATION
17	RC506	TRAINER COMPLETE CONTROLS INSTALLATION
18	RH73	PITOT SYSTEM TOP ASSEMBLY
19	RH125	AFT COCKPIT PITOT SYSTEM INSTALLATION

SCHEMATICS

RA104	AIR CONDITIONING SYSTEM
RH50	PITOT SYSTEM
RQ396	CANOPY JETTISON AND STICK STOWAGE PLUMBING
RQ1026	LOX SYSTEM

SUPPORT EQUIPMENT

RG579	TRAINER HOWDAH ASSEMBLY
RG580	FORWARD AND AFT COCKPIT SERVICE STAND
RG592	UPPER FUSELAGE WEATHER COVER

The two-seat aircraft's drawing tree is simpler only because it does not have to document the operational sensor equipment, and because many of its drawings simply point to the single-seater since the aircraft are generally similar. (U.S. Air Force)

overcame the traditional problem of airborne ELINT where the emitter was required to transmit long enough for the aircraft to move along its track so that the direction-finding process could be completed. Once the North Vietnamese had figured out the length of time it took the Americans to locate their signals, they began to quickly shut down their transmitters. It was generally assumed any future enemy would be at least equally as smart. With at least three ALSS aircraft orbiting in known patterns, the ground station could determine an emitter's position as soon as it came on air, and could relay the location to attacking aircraft.

To flight-test the new system, the remaining seven Air Force U-2C aircraft were equipped with ALSS equipment in 1972. The system encountered serious development problems and it was not until 1975 that an operational test with five U-2Cs was finally conducted in Europe as Exercise CONSTANT TREAT. The results were generally unsatisfactory, but did demonstrate the system had a great deal of potential. The ALSS contract was cancelled, and the Air Force refined and expanded the effort to encompass a larger range of frequencies and signal types. A new PLSS contract was awarded in 1977 to Lockheed Missiles and Space Company.

The initial PLSS equipment was supposed to be ready for flight testing

At the front end of this 20-foot long tailpipe is the F118-GE-101 engine from a U-2S. When the U-2R began to run into performance limitations based on the added weight from new sensors and ECM equipment, Lockheed began to look at a program to re-engine the aircraft similar to the one that had proved so successful on the U-2A/C. The retirement of the last J75-powered fighters from the Air Force hurried this search along, and finally culminated with the General Electric F118 engine being developed for the B-2 stealth bomber program. (Lockheed Martin Skunk Works via Denny Lombard)

aboard an early TR-1A, but development problems meant that the first PLSS-equipped aircraft (Article 074) did not fly until December 1983. A new nose was designed to accommodate the E-Systems ELINT antennas and receivers, while the superpods housed distance measurement equipment and datalinks. More development problems ensued, and it would be another 18 months before a PLSS triad was launched for test missions over NWC China Lake. Although the system was beginning to show promise, the Air Force had lost patience. Other systems, such as the Northrop E-8A Joint STARS, were coming on line that could perform some or all of PLSS's mission. The PLSS lingered on as the Signal Location and Targeting System (SLATS), and was still being tested in a two-aircraft configuration as late as the end of 1987. But time had finally run out, and the program slowly faded from the scene.

Concurrently, Hughes Radar Systems Group was funded to produce

The small wing U-2s did not have a dedicated trainer for the first 17 years, but this was finally rectified by the introduction of the U-2C(T) two-seat conversions in 1972 and 1975. When the original 12 U-2Rs were ordered, no dedicated trainer version was built, and the small wing U-2C(T)s continued to be used. The second batch of big wing U-2s brought two TR-1B trainers (Articles 064 and 065) and a single U-2R(T) (Article 091), allowing the original U-2C(T)s to be retired in 1988. Although the two TR-1Bs were painted white when they were delivered, they later received the same black paint as operational U-2s. (Lockheed Martin Skunk Works via Denny Lombard)

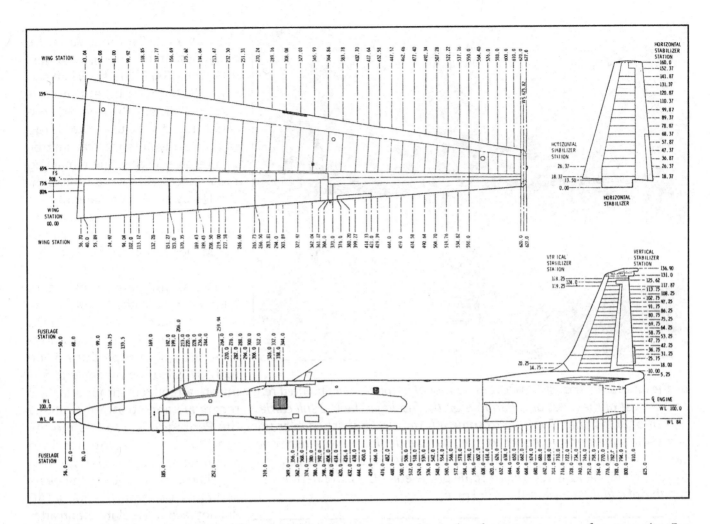

Like all American aircraft, the U-2R/S station numbers are assigned in inches from a common reference point. For the side view, the "zero inch" location is located 68 inches in front of the nose. This allows an air data probe (such as carried by the prototype) to be carried within the same reference system. (U.S. Air Force)

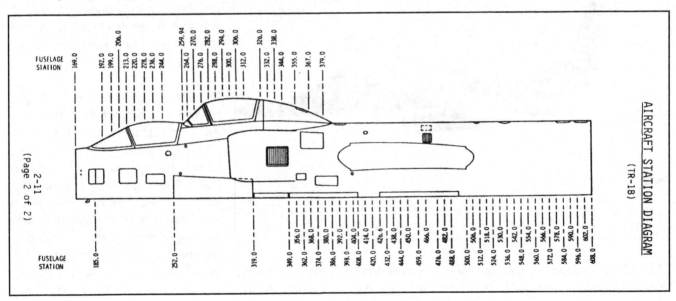

Most of the reference points on the U-2S(T) are the same as the single-seaters, but this drawing shows how they differ around the second cockpit. (U.S. Air Force)

By the late 1990s, the "BB" tail codes and serial numbers were painted red, as are most of the notes and warnings on the fuselage. The U-2 still carries no national insignia. Contrary to some information published over the years, the superpods do not carry fuel, but are dedicated to sensor and electronic equipment. All fuel is carried in the wings and a sump tank under the engine in the fuselage. Unlike some of the early U-2s, the U-2R is not capable of inflight refueling. (U.S. Air Force)

This U-2R is equipped with an optical hatch under the Q-bay. It is becoming less and less frequent that the U-2 is dedicated to traditional film work, the advent of synthetic aperture radar and digital cameras largely supplanting film since it can be relayed in real-time to battlefield commanders. (Lockheed Martin Skunk Works via the Tony Landis Collection)

the Advanced Synthetic Aperture Radar System (ASARS-2). By August 1981 the ASARS-2 radar was flying on a U-2R development aircraft (Article 058) with an extended nose designed to house the large phased-array antenna, transmitter, and receiver/exciter. The remaining radar electronics were housed in the Q-bay, while the datalink was located in the pressurized cavity aft of the tail gear. Fiber-optic cables linked the various components.

The changing environment in Europe would come to Lockheed's rescue however. A perceived need for increased TAC reconnaissance capability in Europe during the mid-1970s led the Air Force to formulate a requirement for a tactical reconnaissance platform. Initially the Pentagon wanted to modify the F-111 tactical fighter into reconnaissance vehicles, an idea that had been proposed ten years earlier by General Dynamics. TAC did not favor this solution, and after exploring other options, concluded that the U-2R would offer several times the F-111's range and loiter capability at only one-third its cost. It also left the F-111 fleet to perform interdiction missions, something it did superbly.

In September 1977 the Pentagon tasked a group of Air Force and Army officers to evaluate the reconnaissance needs for the immediate future. The group concluded that the U-2 was the best platform for PLSS and the ASARS-2. The group also strongly recommended that control of the aircraft be vested in the theater commanders instead of being controlled by the SAC Reconnaissance Center in Omaha. They also did not believe the COMPASS COPE program would produce a tactically useful vehicle in the fore-

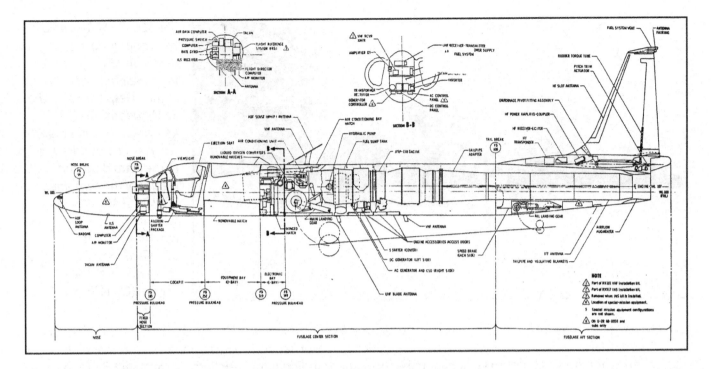

The interior arrangement shows how every usable space has been used by something – HF amplifiers and receivers in the tail, etc. The sensor areas (designated by a "4" within a triangle) are located in the Q-bay and detachable nose sections. The nose breaks at FS169, immediately ahead of the front canopy, while the engine access is provided by separating the rear fuselage at FS608, just ahead of the vertical stabilizer. (U.S. Air Force)

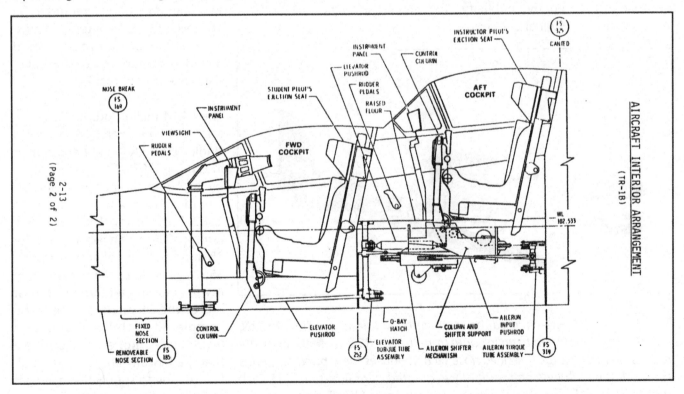

This gives an idea of the modifications done to the flight control system to allow a second set of controls to be installed in the back seat of the U-2S(T). The instructor pilot generally sits in the second seat, which is not equipped with a driftsight. The U-2 flight training accident rate decreased significantly when the first generation two-seaters were introduced, justifying building the four second generation two-seaters. (U.S. Air Force)

The SENIOR SPAN aircraft were operating over Bosnia in January 1998 from their base at Istres, France. Despite its size, the SPAN radome and associated systems only weighs 400 pounds. Due to the extra drag and weight of the combined SENIOR SPAN/SPEAR system, this configuration was the one that benefited most from being reengined with the F118 engine. (Chris Pocock)

seeable future. The report was approved, COMPASS COPE was cancelled, and the FY79 defense budget was changed to provide funds for a restart of the U-2 production line.

Because of the negative publicity surrounding the original U-2 desig-nation, the aircraft was given a new TR-1A designation ("TR" for Tactical Reconnaissance), more in line with its tactical mission. The designation was supposed to prevent news stories that always began "U-2 spy-planes …" – now the stories simply began "TR-1 spyplanes …"

The initial $10.2 million set-up contract called for the reactivation of Air Force Plant No. 42, Site 7 in Palmdale, and the refurbishment of the old U-2R production tooling that had been placed in storage during 1969. New and replacement tooling was manufactured as required. On 16 November 1979, after an almost 12-year lapse, the production of new U-2Rs began, this time in Palmdale instead of Burbank.

The $42.4 million production contract for two Air Force TR-1As and a single NASA ER-2 had been signed in October 1979. This was followed by an Air Force announcement of intentions to buy ten TR-1s during 1982, four during 1983, and five during 1984, with a requirement for 35 at a total cost of approximately $550 million. Interestingly, although it was seldom mentioned, at least ten of the 35 aircraft were to be completed as U-2Rs and funded from "black" money. It is possible that the U.S. intelligence community intended to supply these aircraft to Taiwan, although in the end they were simply absorbed as U.S. assets. Lockheed also discussed the possibility of supplying U-2Rs to the Royal Air Force during 1982 at a

The SENIOR SPUR system used the same antenna fairing as SENIOR SPAN, but this time it was used to uplink data from the ASARS-2 synthetic aperture radar system. The large flat-sided nose section houses the X-band antennas for ASARS- which was operationally evaluated beginning in 1985 with flights from RAF Alconbury. Like most of the later SIGINT payloads, the ASARS-2 system can be remotely operated from ground stations such as TREDS/TRIGS, or the TR-1 ASARS Data Manipulation System (TADMS), which is operated by RAF personnel. (Lockheed Martin Skunk Works via the Tony Landis Collection)

The "generic" nose section of the U-2R/S is little more than an aerodynamic shape with provisions for mounting a 35mm tracking camera. Specialized noses are available for the payloads (sensors) that require them. (U.S. Air Force)

reported unit cost of $20 million, not including sensors, cameras, or ECM equipment.

The steep learning curve that was continuing to be experienced by new Dragon Lady pilots caused the Air Force to purchase two dual control trainers. These TR-1B aircraft were conceptually similar to the two U-2C(T) trainers that were belatedly developed for the small-wing U-2s, and had been serving the U-2R community. The first two-seat TR-1B was completed at Palmdale during January 1983, and following preliminary ground checks, made its first flight on 23 February with Lockheed test pilot Art Peterson at the controls. Unlike the two U-2C(T)s which were modified from U-2C single-seaters, the TR-1Bs were purpose-built with two seats for the training role. A single identical U-2R(T) trainer was also procured using black funding.

By the time production ended, Lockheed had delivered 37 new aircraft. Three two-seat trainers were produced, two TR-1Bs and a single U-2R(T), which were for all intents identical. Thirty-three single-seaters were built – two ER-2s for NASA, seven U-2Rs using black funding, and 25 TR-1As. The 32 Air Force single-seaters were essentially identical, and all TR-1As were redesignated U-2R in October 1991.

Only minor changes were made to the TR-1 compared to the U-2R. The same engine was used, although in

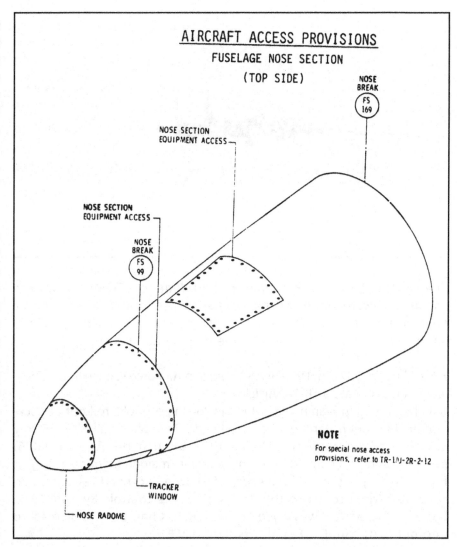

AIRCRAFT ACCESS PROVISIONS
FUSELAGE NOSE SECTION
(TOP SIDE)

NOSE BREAK FS 169

NOSE SECTION EQUIPMENT ACCESS

NOSE SECTION EQUIPMENT ACCESS

NOSE BREAK FS 99

NOTE
For special nose access provisions, refer to TR-1/U-2R-2-12

TRACKER WINDOW

NOSE RADOME

this case the basic engine came from retired F-105 and F-106 fighters and was rebuilt by Pratt & Whitney into the J75-P-13B high-altitude configuration. The most telling external change was the horizontal stabilizer. The original tailplane on the first dozen U-2Rs had needed strengthening, and this was visible as a series of stiffeners which protruded to the exterior surface as small ribs. The new horizontal stabilizers incorporated these stiffeners internally and presented a "clean" external surface. Of course, this difference quickly disappeared since the maintenance personnel routinely swapped rear fuselages between aircraft – a fact that has over the years led to

charges that the Air Force changed aircraft serials numbers. In reality the "different" serial numbers were simply a result of changing rear fuselages between aircraft. When this occurred, parts of the serial numbers were repainted to match whatever airframe the rear fuselage happened to be attached to.

The first of the new aircraft was an ER-2 (Article 063) destined to supplement (and eventually replace) the U-2Cs that were being flown from the Ames Research Center. The first flight was made on 11 May 1981 by Lockheed test pilot Art Peterson, and the aircraft was turned over to NASA on 10 June. It would be followed by a second

The first operational use of the "superpods" was for an E-Systems ELINT system developed in late 1976 under project SENIOR RUBY. The superpods attached to the wing at the same location as the SENIOR SPEAR pods developed earlier, but they were substantially larger. Although the new pods were test-flown from Palmdale in 1975-76, it was not until the mid-1980s that the Air Force asked Lockheed to conduct a full investigation of how these 24-foot long pods changed the flutter characteristics of the aircraft. The pods were found to have minimal effect on the U-2's flutter characteristics, but they did further restrict the aircraft's already limited maneuvering capability.

The SENIOR SPEAR communications intelligence (COMINT) system requires a great many antennas to be fitted to the U-2, mainly under the aft fuselage and superpods. The clean lines of the U-2 were being lost under the array of antennas. (U.S. Air Force via the Tony Landis Collection)

ER-2 (Article 097) in 1989. NASA would also operate a TR-1A (Article 069) beginning in March 1987. This aircraft had been damaged in an accident at RAF Alconbury in October 1983 and was converted to an ER-2 during its repair. NASA returned the aircraft to the Air Force in 1997 while it was being re-engined with the F118 and it is now in Air Force service as a U-2S.

Following a public roll-out at Lockheed's Palmdale facility on 15 July 1981, the first TR-1A (Article 066) made its maiden flight on 1 August 1981 with Lockheed test pilot Ken Weir at the controls. By April 1982, six TR-1As had been delivered to Beale AFB.

In late 1979 the first SENIOR GLASS aircraft (Article 061) was deployed to Europe. In this configuration, the SENIOR RUBY ELINT system was combined with the SENIOR SPEAR COMINT system to produce a versatile collection capability. The classically clean profile of the "jet-powered glider" was no more. Multiple radio monitoring and direction-finding (DF) antennas protruded from the lower fuselage and the superpods, which were now asymmetric since the left pod sported a canoe-type fairing housing parts of the SENIOR SPEAR system. The radio monitoring system used 24 receivers in the HF, VHF, and UHF bands to detect AM, FM, CW, SSB, and WBFM transmissions. The system used highly accurate phase interferometer direction finding, and had automatic scan and reporting capabilities. Operators in a transportable ground control facility with as many as 18 color consoles could specify the search strategies. The air-to-ground datalink was highly directional to prevent detection and jamming, and provided a

Like the SR-71 before it was retired, wherever the U-2 goes, men with M-16 rifles seem to follow. Even at air shows, the U-2s are frequently roped off with guards and small signs that say "Use of deadly force is authorized" – it is generally well advised not to try and get too close. Usually there is no classified equipment on the U-2 when it is at an air show, but the military believes in precautions. (Lockheed Martin)

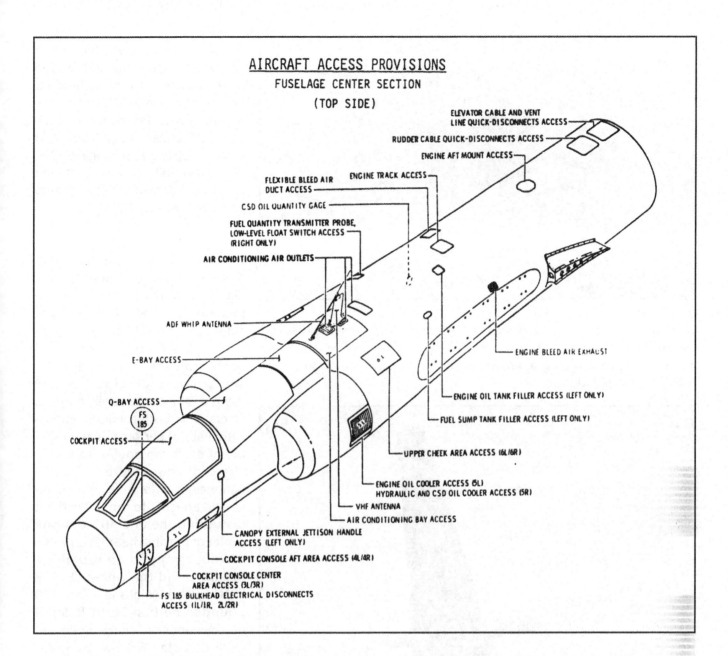

AIRCRAFT ACCESS PROVISIONS
FUSELAGE CENTER SECTION
(TOP SIDE)

ELEVATOR CABLE AND VENT LINE QUICK-DISCONNECTS ACCESS

RUDDER CABLE QUICK-DISCONNECTS ACCESS

ENGINE AFT MOUNT ACCESS

ENGINE TRACK ACCESS

FLEXIBLE BLEED AIR DUCT ACCESS

CSD OIL QUANTITY GAGE

FUEL QUANTITY TRANSMITTER PROBE, LOW-LEVEL FLOAT SWITCH ACCESS (RIGHT ONLY)

AIR CONDITIONING AIR OUTLETS

ADF WHIP ANTENNA

ENGINE BLEED AIR EXHAUST

E-BAY ACCESS

ENGINE OIL TANK FILLER ACCESS (LEFT ONLY)

Q-BAY ACCESS

FS 185

FUEL SUMP TANK FILLER ACCESS (LEFT ONLY)

COCKPIT ACCESS

UPPER CHEEK AREA ACCESS (6L/6R)

ENGINE OIL COOLER ACCESS (5L) HYDRAULIC AND CSD OIL COOLER ACCESS (5R)

VHF ANTENNA

AIR CONDITIONING BAY ACCESS

CANOPY EXTERNAL JETTISON HANDLE ACCESS (LEFT ONLY)

COCKPIT CONSOLE AFT AREA ACCESS (4L/4R)

COCKPIT CONSOLE CENTER AREA ACCESS (3L/3R)

FS 185 BULKHEAD ELECTRICAL DISCONNECTS ACCESS (1L/1R, 2L/2R)

The main fuselage of the U-2R/S, minus the detachable nose and the rear fuselage. This unit is built up as one piece, and includes doors and panels to access the various aircraft systems. All aircraft systems are isolated from the payload compartments in the nose, Q-bay, and superpods, simplifying maintenance. (U.S. Air Force)

full-duplex HF voice capability.

The first operational ASARS-2 sortie was finally flown on 9 July 1985. For the first time, tactical commanders were provided with timely results from an imaging sensor which could operate round- the-clock, with no regard to cloud cover or time of day. By flying above most of the Earth's weather, the aircraft provides the vibration-free platform

demanded by the synthetic X-band radar. The system's SIGINT capability ranges up to 350 miles, although the radar's useful range is about 100 miles less. The aircraft can venture up to 300 miles from the ground station under ideal conditions.

Like the SIGINT sensors, ASARS-2 is controlled from the ground via a wideband real-time datalink. For the European theater, a new TR-1

Exploitation Demonstration System (TREDS) ground station built by Ford Aerospace was set up in trailers at a former missile maintenance facility near Hahn AB, Germany. Codenamed METRO TANGO, this interim system was scheduled to be replaced by two fully hardened TR-1 Ground Station (TRIGS) underground bunkers, but the first TRIGS was never completed due to the end of the Cold War. Ground force

Site 2 at Air Force Plant 42 in Palmdale, California, is the home to U-2 heavy maintenance conducted by Lockheed. This photo shows five U-2Rs and three SR-71s undergoing maintenance or modification during the late 1980s. (Lockheed Martin)

commanders were excited by the new capabilities, but demanded more flexible methods of distributing the data, and the U.S. Army subsequently had Westinghouse develop the Tactical Radar Correlator (TRAC) mobile ground station. TRAC is an air-mobile 40-foot container that can operate independently from the fixed-site TREDS/TRIGS.

Getting real-time data to force commanders, both locally and at U.S. locations, continued to be a high priority for the reconnaissance programs. In 1985 the Air Force authorized the SENIOR SPAN satellite datalink program for the U-2. Lockheed worked with E-Systems and Unisys to develop a system using a 30-inch parabolic antenna steerable in both azimuth and elevation at 60° per second and capable of elevation angles up to 85°. The challenges were to build a lightweight radome for the antenna and attach it to the U-2 without disrupting the aircraft's delicate center of gravity. The solution was a 17-foot long pod on top of the fuselage, and the whole SENIOR SPAN system weighs less than 400 pounds. The first SENIOR SPAN deployment with a fully-configured U-2R (Article 053) was to South Korea in late 1988, with the first European deployment following in March 1989.

(text continued on page 69)

A relatively cleanly configured U-2R banks away. The object sticking out sideways from the canopy area is the rear-view mirror, a useful device for checking to see if you are leaving contrails at 70,000 feet. Contrails are not a desirable trait since they can be spotted many miles away, and U-2s will frequently adjust their altitude slightly to try and eliminate them. (Lockheed Martin)

THE LADY SHOWS HER COLORS

NOT ALWAYS BLACK OR WHITE

Initially, all small wing U-2s were delivered in natural metal finish. The U-2Ds and other U-2s based at Edwards frequently sported day-glo trim, or in the case of the MIDAS experiments, had various portions of the wings and fuselage painted black. In 1961-62 the Air Force aircraft were repainted in a high-gloss light grey. Various schemes to reduce the visibility of the U-2, including polka dots and zebra stripes, were flight tested over Edwards, but none proved terribly effective. The CIA decided to paint their aircraft a very dark "midnight blue" since it would blend into the dark sky that is prevalent at high altitude, and the Air Force began to follow in 1964. In many photographs this particular shade of blue takes an an almost glossy sheen.

The first ER-2 flies in formation with one of NASA's U-2Cs over the Golden Gate Bridge. Until 1997, the U-2s were based at NASA's Ames Research Center at Moffett Field, at the south end of the Bay. (NASA/DFRC via Tony Landis)

The U-2 used a control wheel instead of the stick used in most high performance aircraft. It was felt the wheel was easier to manipulate while wearing the pressure suit gloves on long flights. The driftsight dominates the forward instrument panel. Noteworthy are the two pencils in their holders on the control wheel. (NASA/DFRC via Tony Landis)

In late 1965 the Pittsburgh Paint and Glass Company devised the BLACK VELVET flat black paint that would become standard on the U-2. There are reports that this paint makes some contribution to reducing the aircraft's radar return by using microscopic ferrous particles to suppress side lobes. Extremely small balls of glass are also embedded in the paint to soak up light and suppress reflections in the visible spectrum. At the same time that the fleet was painted in BLACK VELVET, the sunshield over the canopy was repainted black instead of white. In the early 1970s, when the last U-2Cs were deployed to England to test ALSS, the British government request a "less sinister" paint scheme, and the two-tone grey camouflage was applied to all remaining U-2Cs.

A technician stands in the cockpit while he works on the structure in the Q-bay. The construction of the U-2 was for the most part conventional and conservative. The exception was the omission of ribs in the wings, making them somewhat fragile and difficult to manufacture. (Lockheed Martin Skunk Works via Denny Lombard)

By the late 1980s the U-2 had not only become a frequent attraction at air shows, but the squadrons had begun to sell souvenirs. This Dragon Lady emblem was on the back of tee-shirts being sold by the detachment at Patrick AFB, Florida, in the early 1990s. (Dragon Lady Handlers via Dennis R. Jenkins)

The first U-2R (Article 051) made its maiden flight in natural metal finish. The standard optical nose (not the camera windows) was fitted although it contained flight test instrumentation connected to the alpha/beta boom. This aircraft spent the first year of testing unpainted. (Lockheed Martin Skunk Works via the Tony Landis Collection)

WARBIRD**TECH**
SERIES

When first seen, the large SENIOR SPAN antenna fairing was believed to contain some form of airborne early warning radar that would enable the U-2 to serve as a mini-AWACS. In fact, the fairing houses the satellite communications antenna that allows SIGINT and other intelligence to be relayed in real-time to whomever needs it on the ground. The

white streaks on the antenna fairing and vertical stabilizer are cotton puffs, used during flight testing to determine the airflow characteristics. This was an early evaluation flight from Palmdale and the radome probably does not contain any operational equipment. (Lockheed Martin Skunk Works via the Tony Landis Collection)

The superpods on the wings significantly change the look of the U-2R, but fortunately they have little impact on its handling or performance. Although the initial years of service were flown without the superpods, today almost all missions require superpods of some description – and many different varieties exist depending upon the sensor payload. (Lockheed Martin)

At least two early U-2s were based at Edwards for experiments, some classified, and some not. Beginning in the mid 1960s the U-2s frequently flew during the annual Edwards air show. Here is Article 368 (56-6701) as it taxis past the crowd. (Mick Roth Collection)

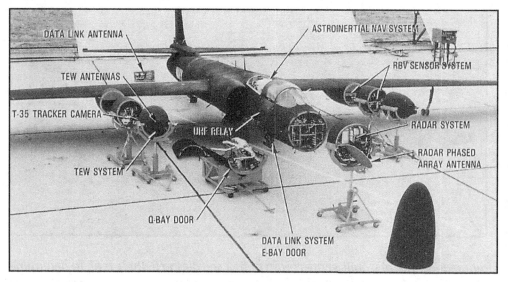

Labels: DATA LINK ANTENNA, ASTROINERTIAL NAV SYSTEM, TEW ANTENNAS, RBV SENSOR SYSTEM, T-35 TRACKER CAMERA, UHF RELAY, RADAR SYSTEM, TEW SYSTEM, RADAR PHASED ARRAY ANTENNA, Q-BAY DOOR, DATA LINK SYSTEM E-BAY DOOR

The Navy's EP-X project used two U-2Rs borrowed from the CIA to test an experimental sea surveillance system. These were amongst the first big wing U-2s to use sensor pods on the wings, although they were decidedly smaller than the eventual "superpods" and did not require the flaps be modified. This graphic depicts the location of the EP-X equipment on the U-2R. (U.S. Navy)

It was fairly unusual to see a natural metal U-2C except while they were undergoing maintenance, and then they did not carry markings. Article 374 (56-6707) appears to be a fairly late U-2C with the full length "canoe" on top of the fuselage and slipper tanks on the wings. The rear portion of the canoe was fiberglass, hence the light grey paint. (Mick Roth Collection)

Two of the Air Force Flight Test Center's U-2s fly over the Edwards' flightline. The furthest aircraft is Article 368 (56-6701) which is was later retired to the SAC Museum at Offutt AFB. The aircraft in the foreground is Article 389 (56-6722) configured with a turret containing sensors as part of the MIDAS satellite program. It was later retired to the Air Force Museum at Wright-Patterson AFB, Ohio, where it was reconfigured as a U-2A. (U.S. Air Force via the Tony Landis Collection)

WARBIRDTECH
SERIES

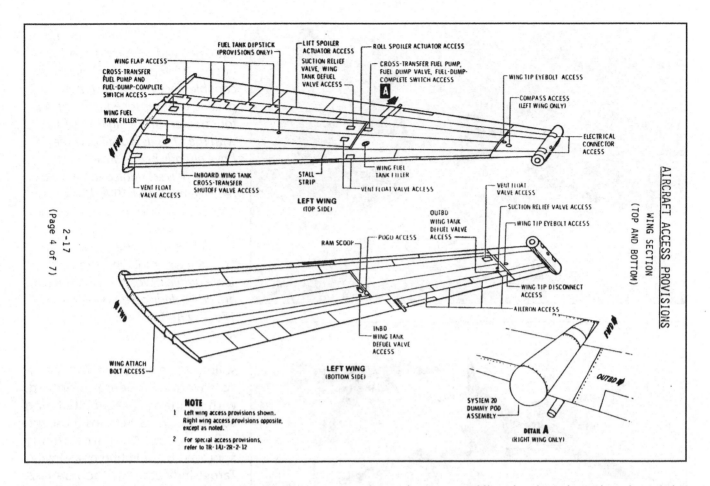

All of the U-2R/S's fuel is contained in integral wing tanks, with separate fillers for the inboard tank and the outboard tank. No fuel is contained within the foldable sections. Four segment flaps and ailerons are installed on the trailing edge. The System 20 infrared detection system is installed in a small fairing on the right wing's trailing edge. During the late 1990s, a similar fairing was added to the left wing to contain a GPS antenna. (U.S. Air Force)

(text continued from page 64) The SENIOR YEAR Electro-optical Reconnaissance System (SYERS) evolved during the late 1970s from photo reconnaissance satellites which relayed digitized imagery to ground stations for processing. This was possible by replacing the traditional film with light-sensitive charged-coupled devices (CCD) which captured the images as digital data. A digital camera was developed for the U-2 by Itek, a division of Litton which had dominated spy satellite optics for many years. When Itek first presented the concept to Lockheed, it assumed that the new camera would replace the existing film camera in the Q-bay. This would have entailed designing a new Q-bay optical hatch, but Lockheed decided to dust off drawings for a rotating nose section which had been designed to house a sensor for tracking reentry vehicles. This had been an early proposed use for the U-2R, but had not been pursued. The first four feet of the SENIOR OPEN nose has a single optical glass aperture which is rotated by a servo to "look" left, right, or below the aircraft flight path. A complex system of mirrors is housed behind the glass, while the camera's body remains stationary in the fixed nose section.

After flight tests, the first SYERS was deployed for operational testing in Korea where a ground station had already been established for ASARS-2 operations. The ground portion of SYERS is codenamed SENIOR BLADE, and performs functions similar to the ASARS-2 ground station: control of the sensor, processing, display, and distribution of the imagery. If the sensor is within line-of-sight (about 220 miles) of the ground station, the aircraft is "on-tether" and relays the imagery in real-time. If the aircraft is beyond the range of the ground station, SYERS stores the information onboard then relays it when the U-2 is again within range.

Cameras were back in vogue to some extent after DESERT STORM, and the venerable Type-H camera was improved by incorporating

The TR-1B/U-2R(T) aircraft are not equipped with superpods, and are not considered operationally capable since the Q-bay is not available for sensor equipment. All four trainers are being re-engined with the F118 as U-2S(T)s. Three have already been converted, and the fourth is scheduled to be redelivered in mid-1998. The fourth trainer, unlike the first three, was not built as a two-seater. A single-seat TR-1A that was damaged in an accident was modified into a two-seater while it was being repaired to provide a dedicated trainer for the 17th RW at RAF Alconbury. (Lockheed Martin)

Three U-2Rs pose for a staged photo at Beale AFB. The SR-71 hangers are in the upper left, and a TR-1B/U-2R(T) is across from them. The center aircraft is configured with the Precision Location Strike System (PLSS), while the other two have generic noses and superpods. An outgrowth of the earlier ALSS, the PLSS was intended to use three TR-1s flying race-track patterns near the front lines of a European land war, but ran into serious development problems. It has been abandoned in favor of the Northrop Joint STARS program that uses modified Boeing 707 airframes. (Lockheed Martin)

solid-state electronics. Other sensors were also being improved, with an infrared capability being added to SYERS. Perhaps most significant, the Air Force finally approved the addition of a Moving Target Indicator (MTI) to ASARS-2. Testing was completed in October 1991, and the ASARS-2/MTI became operational in 1995.

For years, the Litton LN-33 P2/P3 Inertial Navigation System was used by the U-2, periodically updated by the Northrop NAS-21 astro-inertial star-tracker originally developed for the Blackbirds. The advent of the Global Positioning System (GPS) allowed Lockheed to replace the excellent, but complicated, NAS-21 with a lightweight GPS receiver faired into the U-2's left wing trailing edge.

When the final General Dynamics F-106 Delta Dart was retired, the U-2R became the last user of the Pratt & Whitney J75, and the engine's support costs threatened to become uneconomical. Moreover, in a repeat of the small-wing U-2's history, the weight of new

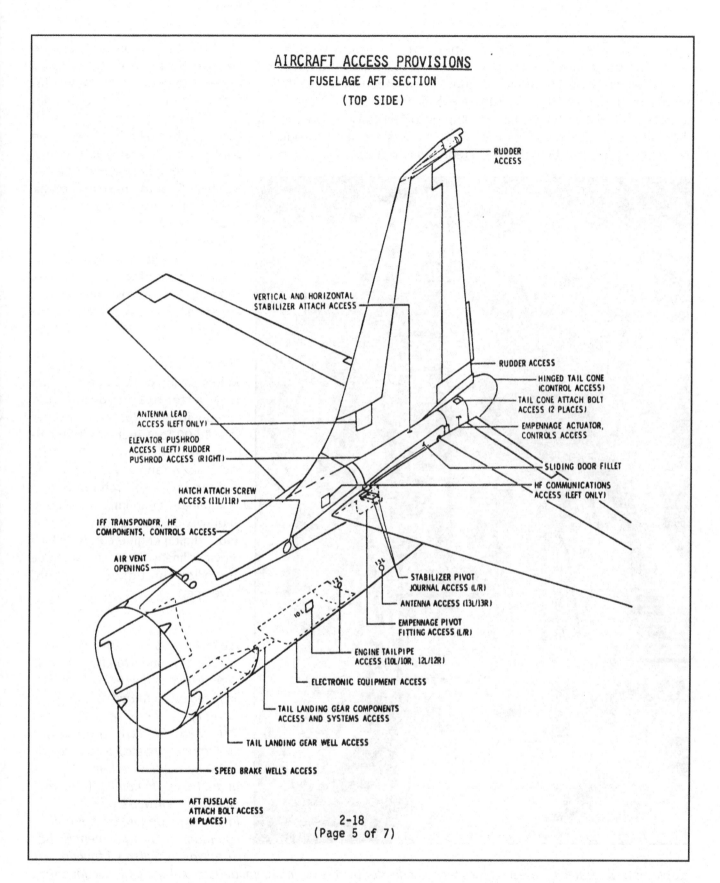

AIRCRAFT ACCESS PROVISIONS
FUSELAGE AFT SECTION
(TOP SIDE)

RUDDER ACCESS

VERTICAL AND HORIZONTAL STABILIZER ATTACH ACCESS

RUDDER ACCESS

HINGED TAIL CONE (CONTROL ACCESS)

TAIL CONE ATTACH BOLT ACCESS (2 PLACES)

EMPENNAGE ACTUATOR, CONTROLS ACCESS

ANTENNA LEAD ACCESS (LEFT ONLY)

ELEVATOR PUSHROD ACCESS (LEFT) RUDDER PUSHROD ACCESS (RIGHT)

SLIDING DOOR FILLET

HF COMMUNICATIONS ACCESS (LEFT ONLY)

HATCH ATTACH SCREW ACCESS (11L/11R)

IFF TRANSPONDER, HF COMPONENTS, CONTROLS ACCESS

AIR VENT OPENINGS

STABILIZER PIVOT JOURNAL ACCESS (L/R)

ANTENNA ACCESS (13L/13R)

EMPENNAGE PIVOT FITTING ACCESS (L/R)

ENGINE TAILPIPE ACCESS (10L/10R, 12L/12R)

ELECTRONIC EQUIPMENT ACCESS

TAIL LANDING GEAR COMPONENTS ACCESS AND SYSTEMS ACCESS

TAIL LANDING GEAR WELL ACCESS

SPEED BRAKE WELLS ACCESS

AFT FUSELAGE ATTACH BOLT ACCESS (4 PLACES)

2-18
(Page 5 of 7)

The aft fuselage of the U-2R/S is held to the forward fuselage by four 5/8-inch bolts. This is an improvement over the small wing U-2s, which only used three bolts. Surprisingly, this seems to be more than sufficient. Various antennas, receivers, and exciters (transmitters) are installed in locations in the aft fuselage and tail. (U.S. Air Force)

sensor and datalink systems was restricting the aircraft's operating performance. Lockheed selected the General Electric F118-GE-101 turbofan (called the F101-GE-F29 at the time) as a replacement for the J75. The engine was being developed for the then still-secret Northrop B-2 stealth bomber and developed 18,300 lbf while offering a significant weight reduction and improved fuel consumption. And it fit. The re-engined aircraft would be redesignated U-2S.

A refurbished ground test engine from the B-2 program was released to Skunk Works in 1988 and was fitted to a test aircraft (Article 090) which made its first flight with Lockheed test pilot Ken Weir at the controls on 23 May 1989. Oddly, this was four months before the B-2 first flew. Over the next 15 months, 82 flight hours were logged. Initial flights were limited to engine-out gliding distance of Edwards AFB, because, unlike the J75 turbojet, the new turbofan could not be restarted in flight by wind-milling. An emergency air-start system was developed for the production U-2S.

The flight test results showed a weight saving of 1,300 pounds and 16% better fuel economy compared with the J75. This translates to a 3,500 foot increase in maximum altitude and a 1,400 mile increase in range. Other benefits include increased reliability and maintainability, an improved center of gravity due to the lighter engine, and a digital engine control which provides linear thrust with stall-free operation throughout the flight envelope.

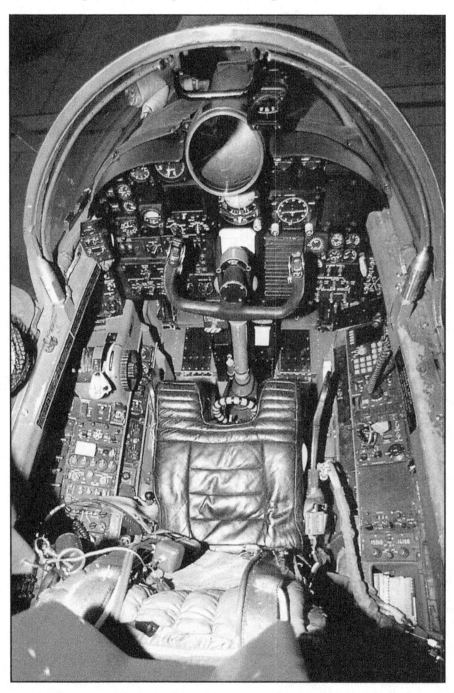

While the F118 engine is being installed, the opportunity is taken to slightly update the U-2 cockpit. This included an upgraded caution & warning panel, new engine instruments (N2, EGT, Oil Pressure, Oil Temperature, etc.), better fuel instruments (fuel totalizer, quantity/time remaining, burn rate, etc.), and improved air data instruments. Updated radios and communications equipment is also installed. A small multi-function display is now located to the left of the attitude indicator, but the large circular driftscope display still occupies the top center. Noteworthy is the fan installed on the canopy (barely visible at left). Although not useful for operational missions where the pilot is in a full pressure suit, the fan provides some additional cabin air circulation when pilots are wearing normal flight suits during relatively low altitude flights. (Lockheed Martin)

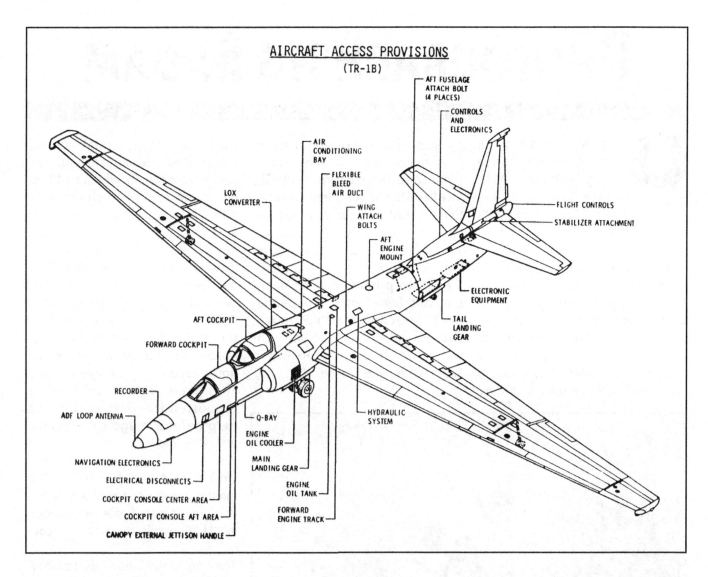

AIRCRAFT ACCESS PROVISIONS
(TR-1B)

Many access panels are provided on the U-2 to allow maintenance personnel to service and check the systems while the aircraft is on the ground. The U-2S(T) is generally similar to the U-2R/S except for the second cockpit installed in the Q-bay and a lack of operational systems (ECM, cameras, etc.) (U.S. Air Force)

The initial production U-2S conversion (Article 071) first flew on 12 August 1994 and the first three conversions were handed back to the Air Force during a delivery ceremony on 28 October 1994. One of these aircraft (Article 078) had been delivered as a single-seat TR-1A but severely damaged at Alconbury on 24 April 1990. The aircraft was subsequently placed in storage at Palmdale, and was rebuilt as a two-seat TU-2S.

All remaining U-2s, including the four of the original 12 U-2Rs built in 1967-68, will be re-engined by the end of 1998. At the same time, wiring, and mounting provisions are being standardized, so that each aircraft will be capable of carrying the entire inventory of sensors. The fatigue life of the U-2R was originally envisioned as 20,000 hours, but in August 1994 the first aircraft (Article 060) passed that milestone without problem, and a new limit of 30,000 hours has been set.

In recent years a great deal of money has been diverted to fund the accelerated development of a new generation of Unmanned Aerial Vehicles (UAV) such as Tier 3-Minus. It is claimed the UAVs are capable of performing the U-2's mission, but a debate has raged over their utility, maturity, and total cost. Observers with long memories can recall the same debate over the relative merits of COMPASS COPE and the U-2 in the mid-1970s. Meanwhile, the U-2 is as busy as ever. Unfortunately, five U-2Rs have been lost in accidents during the last five years, reducing the fleet to 30 operational U-2s, plus four trainers, and the two ER-2s.

PHOTOGRAPHING SADAM

On 1 October 1981 the 17th Reconnaissance Wing and the 95th Reconnaissance Squadron were formed and on 12 February 1983 the first European-based TR-1A (Article 068) was flown from Beale to RAF Alconbury. This 6,000 miles flight logged nearly 14 hours of flight time. For the first two years of its existence, the 17th RW had only three TR-1As and nine pilots, but by 1985 had 12 aircraft along with 500 support personnel. New facilities were built as Alconbury, including 13 unique hardened wide-span aircraft shelters and a hardened maintenance facility known as MAGIC MOUNTAIN. The Air Force reported that the RAF Alconbury operation cost approximately $1 million per year, a questionably low figure. With Alconbury established, the U-2 had two primary bases (Alconbury and Beale), plus semi-permanent detachments in Panama, Cyprus, and Korea. Later, detachments would be established in Saudi Arabia and France.

On 19 June 1961, a small country called Kuwait declared its independence from Britain, which had held it as a protectorate since 1899. Although only 900 square miles in area, Kuwait holds rich oil reserves, making it strategically important to most of the world. By July 1990, Iraq's Sadam Hussein let the world know that he intended to annex Kuwait. At 01:00 on 2 August 1990 the Iraqi army stormed across the border with Kuwait, and within six hours occupied the entire country. Four days later Saudi Arabia requested the United States to help defend it against possible attack by Iraq.

On 7 August 1990 two U-2Rs (designations present a problem here - the aircraft from Beale were generally U-2Rs, while those from Alcon-

This Iraqi airfield shows the result of precision-guided munition strikes to aircraft holding areas and some operations buildings. This image was taken by an HR-329 Type-H camera from an altitude of approximately 70,000 feet. The Hycon-manufactured Type-H has become the main film camera of modern U-2 operations, finally replacing the faithful Type-B. The high-resolution gyro-stabilized camera has a 66-inch focal length lens and was first introduced on the U-2C in 1965. The Type-H was meant to be used at slant distances from the target (as in this photograph), but during DESERT STORM some missions were flown with it shooting at nadir. (Coy F. Cross II, 9th RW History Office)

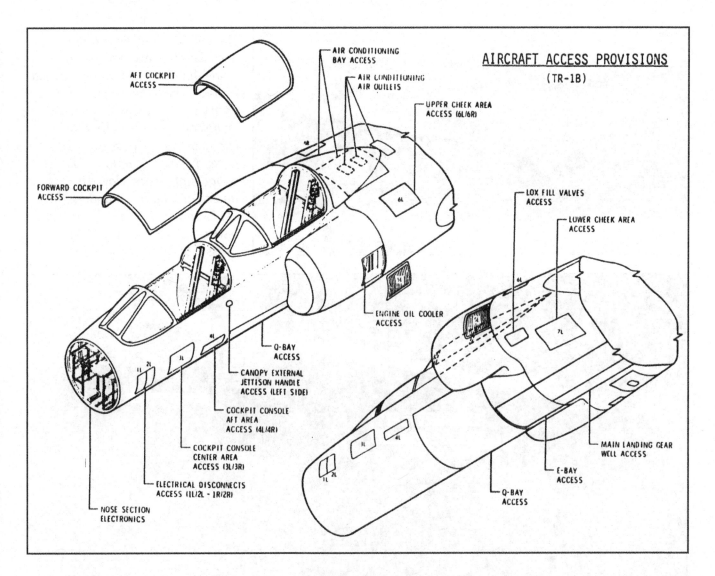

Liquid Oxygen (LOX) is used by the U-2 to provide breathing air for the pilot(s) at high altitude. The dewar is filled using a small access panel under the left air intake. The engine oil coolers for the U-2R/S are located behind flush grills on the side of the air intakes, replacing the large, drag inducing, scoop used on the U-2C. (U.S. Air Force)

bury were TR-1A – I'll call them all U-2Rs) were ordered to Saudi Arabia, and ten days later the aircraft arrived at Taif, beginning the Dragon Lady's involvement in the Gulf War.

Just getting to Saudi Arabia took some doing. No contingency plan existed for a deployment to the Middle East, and the massive effort to reinforce Saudi Arabia meant airlift capacity was in short supply. The two U-2s needed 21 officers, 120 enlisted personnel, and 25 Lockheed contractors to begin opera-

tions. They also needed their special JP-TS fuel, and the nearest supply was at RAF Akrotiri and Torrejon AB, Spain. As a temporary measure, three 55,000 gallon rubber bladders were flown to Taif, and KC-10s and C-141s carried 3,000 55-gallon drums of JP-TS to fill them. This constituted a three week supply. Continued airlift brought this up to a six week supply, after which fuel was brought in by ship to Jeddah and trucked to Taif.

The first two U-2Rs landed at King Fahad AB in Taif on 17 August 1990

as the first contingent of OL-CH, later designated as 1704th Reconnaissance Squadron (Provisional). Two days later OL-CH launched its first two OLYMPIC FLARE sorties. The initial tracks were in the neutral zone between Iraq, Saudi Arabia, and Kuwait, 15–20 miles south of the Iraqi border. From there the U-2s could survey most of southern Iraq, including Baghdad. A few days later the tracks expanded along the Saudi-Iraqi border, the Saudi-Kuwaiti border, and the Saudi–Yemen border.

The SENIOR YEAR Electro-optical Reconnaissance System (SYERS) made this image of burning Kuwaiti oil fields. The flame and smoke from each well are clearly visible. SYERS is an Itek digital camera that uses charged-coupled devices (CCD) instead of film to capture a digital image that can be relayed in real-time to ground commanders. The SYERS camera is generally carried in a special nose on the U-2R. (Coy F. Cross II, 9th RW History Office)

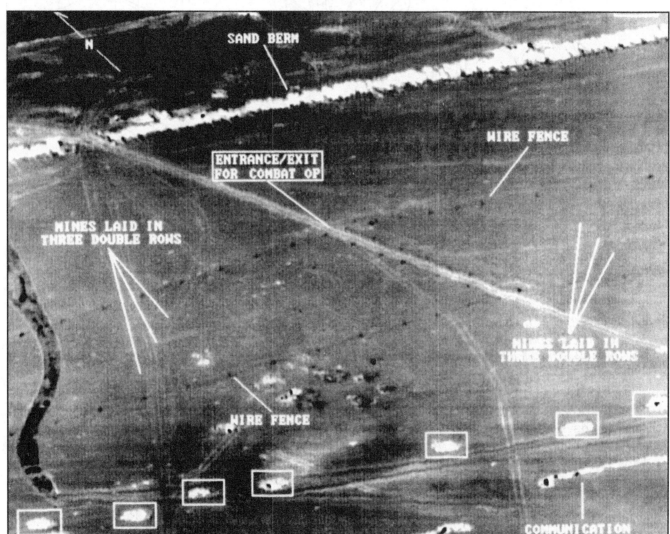

The Advanced Synthetic Aperture Radar System (ASARS-2) proved to be extremely useful in the Gulf War, especially after the Iraqis set the oil wells on fire and obscured the battlefield from traditional cameras. Here ASARS-2 shows a multi-layered Iraqi defense position, with annotations provided by analysts on the ground after they reviewed the data in near-real-time. The fact that ASARS-2 can detect and map items such as barbed-wire fences and land mine positions makes it a very useful tool. ASARS-2 does not operate in the visible electromagnetic spectrum, meaning it can penetrate clouds, smoke, and darkness. (Coy F. Cross II, 9th RW History Office)

Even the "generic" U-2R/S nose contains a great many antenna locations, plus the glazed glass window for the 35mm tracking camera. Systems can use these antenna locations as needed, although most of the specialized systems carried today (ASARS-2, etc.) have their own custom nose sections tailored to their specific needs. (U.S. Air Force)

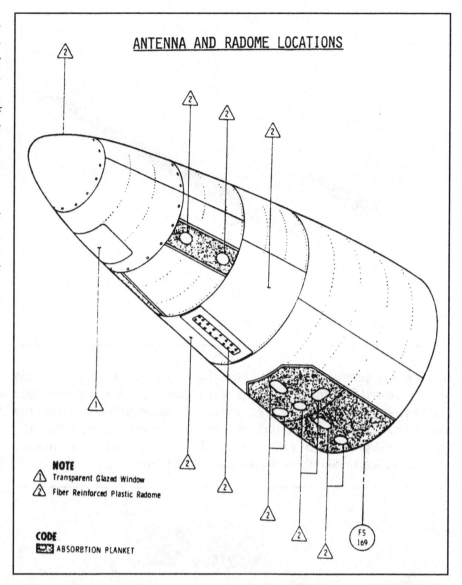

ANTENNA AND RADOME LOCATIONS

NOTE
1. Transparent Glazed Window
2. Fiber Reinforced Plastic Radome

CODE
▨ ABSORBTION PLANKET

FS 169

The first aircraft deployed to Taif was equipped with SYERS, although the infrared sensor was not operational during the Gulf War. The SENIOR BLADE van arrived in Saudi Arabia on 13 August 1990, but because Taif was considered too far from Iraq, the van was deployed to Riyadh to give SYERS maximum time "on-tether" while patrolling along the Saudi-Iraqi border. The real-time SYERS imagery allowed commanders to dynamically assess the situation on display terminals. After DESERT STORM began, and the U-2s began flying over Iraq, a second SENIOR BLADE van (dubbed Son-of-Blade) was deployed to King Khalid Military City (KKMC) near the border. This allowed SYERS to cover nearly all of southern Iraq while remaining on-tether.

The other electronic imagery system, ASARS-2, came to the desert on 23 August with two TR-1As from Alconbury. Unlike SYERS and the cameras, ASARS-2 could "see through" smoke, dust, and darkness. The Army's Tactical Radar Correlator (TRAC) van was set up in the same compound in Riyadh as the SENIOR BLADE van. The imagery data was relayed directly to the TRAC van where intelligence officers used the information to direct airborne strike aircraft to targets. Neither the TRAC nor SENIOR BLADE vans had completed opera-

tional evaluation and testing when they deployed to Saudi Arabia, but both performed admirably.

In December 1990 the 9th RW moved the Mobile Intelligence Processing Element (MIPE), a deployable ground station housed in 15 environmentally controlled vans, to Riyadh. Originally designed for the SR-71, the MIPE lost its funding when the SR-71 was retired and was put into storage at Beale AFB. The system was kept from falling into disrepair, but could not be properly maintained due to lack of funds. In September-October 1990, the Defense Intelligence Agency

asked if the MIPE could deploy to Saudi Arabia. After assessing the MIPE, 9th RW officials explained that the system would need at least 14 days of contract maintenance before it could be operational. Eventually the Air Force Logistics Command authorized the needed maintenance, but only allowed six days before deployment to Riyadh on 19 December. The first IRIS-III mission was on 31 December 1990 and MIPE personnel processed the film on 1 January 1991.

The limiting operational factor in the U-2R inventory has always been the sensors. There are only a certain

The landing gear configuration of the U-2 shows up well here. The main gear is located forward and consists of two pneumatic tires. The rear gear uses two solid-polyurethane tires, and caused some problems during the Gulf War. A "pogo" is used to support each wing while the aircraft is on the ground, with the pogos falling off as the aircraft leaves the runway. (Lockheed Martin Skunk Works via Denny Lombard)

number of each type of sensor. Each aircraft carried the necessary wiring to accommodate a certain subset of the available sensors. As the aircraft inventory increased at Taif, maintenance personal often switched sensors between aircraft. The exception was that only one aircraft (Article 070) was equipped to carry the SENIOR SPAN satellite system. Lockheed was quickly ordered to convert a second aircraft to carry the system, and it deployed late in the Gulf War. This situation came about since the sensors that equip the U-2s in the 1990s were not even envisioned when the aircraft were built. The U-2S modification program is correcting this limitation, and all aircraft will be capable of carrying all sensor packages.

By the end of August 1990, OL-CH had flown eleven SYERS, seven SENIOR SPAN, and three ASARS-2 missions for a total of 168.9 hours. Initially the U-2s flew without escort, but after two Iraqi fighters tailed a U-2 flight on 14 September, Coalition fighters were dispatched with most future missions to provide a MiGCAP. During DESERT STORM, over 20 U-2 flights were tracked by Iraqi fighters or ground radar sites, but no hostile action was taken against the spyplanes.

A problem with tail-wheel tires illustrated the close relationship between the civilian contractors and the U-2 military maintainers. The U-2's rear tires are solid, not

These three ASARS-2 equipped U-2Rs are seen on the ramp at Lockheed's Palmdale facility after returning from the Gulf War. Three more U-2s are in the hanger in the background. The ASARS-2 nose has a distinctive scoop on top that ducts air to the heat exchanger used to control the temperature of the systems inside. A large antenna occupies most of the nose, while mission electronics sit in the back third of the nose. (Lockheed Martin Skunk Works via Denny Lombard)

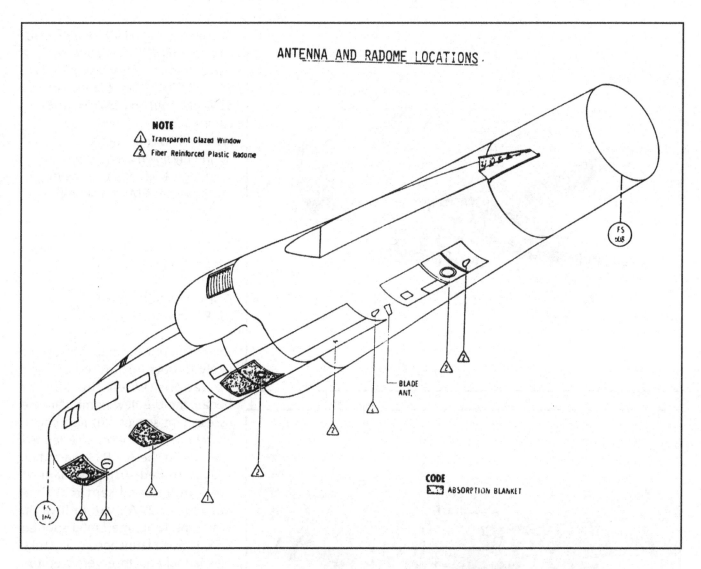

ANTENNA AND RADOME LOCATIONS.

NOTE
⚠1 Transparent Glazed Window
⚠2 Fiber Reinforced Plastic Radome

BLADE ANT.

CODE
☒ ABSORPTION BLANKET

The bottom of the fuselage also has several antennas located on it, most of these for communication radios, ECM systems, or air traffic control transponders. The driftsight optical port is located forward. (U.S. Air Force)

pneumatic like most aircraft tires, and in the 1970s more durable polyurethane tires replaced the original rubber tires. The polyurethane worked well until 1990 when the tread started separating from the tire carcass. At Taif, where the aircraft sometimes had to taxi for a long distance, the U-2 would arrive at the end of the runway, ready for takeoff, with a separated rear tire. Working together, the civilian and military maintainers developed a technique for changing the tire with the aircraft engine running, preventing late takeoffs. Although the tire manu-

facturer denied any change in the manufacturing process, the problem was eventually discovered. Environmental concerns had caused the manufacturer to replace aerosol cans of 5% silicon, used as a separating agent in the tire molds, with a 100% silicon solution applied with a cloth. The higher concentration of silicon prevented the polyurethane from adhering properly. Switching from silicon to Teflon solved the problem.

Tankers from the 9th RW were also critical to the U-2's success during the Gulf War. The KC-135Qs had

originally been assigned to the 9th RW to support the SR-71 Blackbirds. Although the Military Airlift Command activated the Civil Reserve Air Fleet (CRAF) for the first time in history to provide additional capacity, airlift was still very limited. The U-2s used normal airlift where feasible, but the 20 9th RW tankers deployed to Jeddah carried almost all U-2 parts, equipment, and people between Beale, Alconbury, and Taif. One KC-135Q even carried a spare J75 engine to Taif, a feat few people believed possible. Tankers also shifted sensors between Korea, Panama, England, Cyprus, Saudi

Article 060 (68-10338) configured to carry the SENIOR SPAN antenna pod on top of the fuselage, plus the SENIOR GLASS (combination of SENIOR SPEAR and SENIOR RUBY) communications intelligence systems. This configuration is frequently flown over Bosnia to monitor the U.N.-brokered cease fire. (Lockheed Martin Skunk Works via Denny Lombard)

Arabia, and the United States to support operations as needed.

During DESERT SHIELD the U-2 looked for indications that Iraqi troops were moving, especially toward Saudi Arabia, and sought likely targets for future bombing operations. When the air war began, the U-2 flew bomb damage assessment sorties, but also began searching for Scud missile launch sites. Using the ASARS-2 on-tether, U-2s patrolled suspected launch areas in Iraq and sent real-time data to the TRAC van in Riyadh. When the TRAC interpreter spotted a likely Scud launcher, an air strike was launched. Observers credited this technique with destroying 15 or 16 missile launchers during the first week of the war. Later, a B-52 bombardier joined the TRAC crew to help assess targets. On one mission, the ASARS-2 information was used to redirect B-52s already in

Many of the U-2s operating out of the country (particularly with the 17th RW in England) carried tail art. Here Article 070 (80-1070) is fully configured as a SENIOR GLASS/SENIOR SPAN aircraft. (Lockheed Martin)

The combination of SENIOR GLASS (which itself is a combination of SENIOR SPEAR and SENIOR RUBY) and the satellite antenna has proven popular with field commanders, as well as their political leaders back home. This setup is capable of gathering a great deal of communication intelligence from locations far enough afield to avoid any great possibility of getting shot down. The aircraft is somewhat less happy since it is carrying a great deal more weight and drag than it was designed for, although the F118 engine has helped the situation somewhat. (Lockheed Martin)

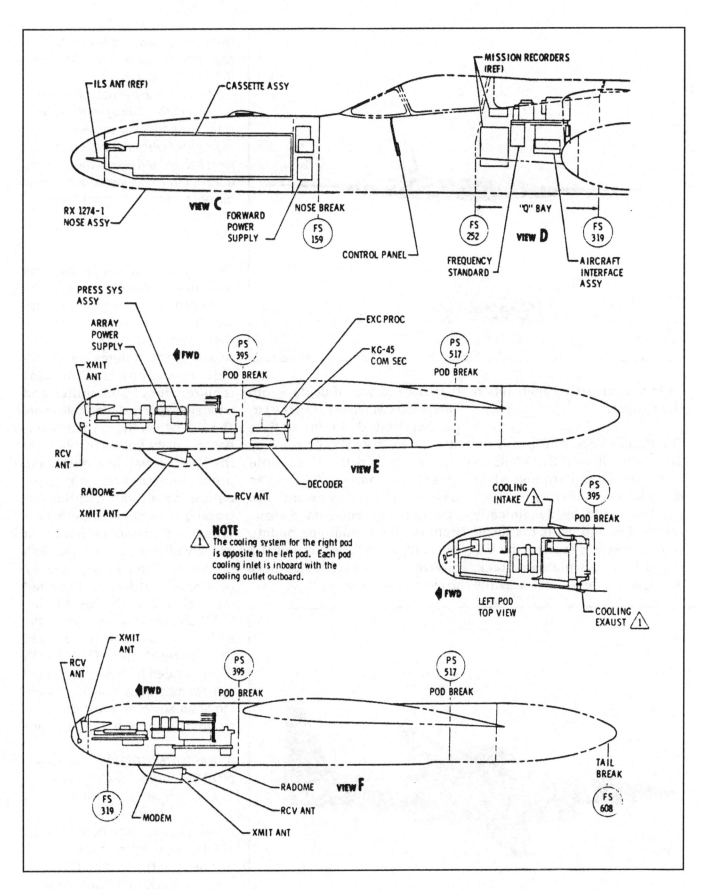

ILS ANT (REF)
CASSETTE ASSY
MISSION RECORDERS (REF)

RX 1274-1 NOSE ASSY
VIEW C
FORWARD POWER SUPPLY
NOSE BREAK
FS 159
CONTROL PANEL
FS 252
FREQUENCY STANDARD
"Q" BAY
VIEW D
FS 319
AIRCRAFT INTERFACE ASSY

PRESS SYS ASSY
ARRAY POWER SUPPLY
XMIT ANT
FWD
PS 395
POD BREAK
EXC PROC
KG-45 COM SEC
PS 517
POD BREAK

RCV ANT
RADOME
XMIT ANT
RCV ANT
DECODER
VIEW E

NOTE
1 The cooling system for the right pod is opposite to the left pod. Each pod cooling inlet is inboard with the cooling outlet outboard.

COOLING INTAKE 1
PS 395
POD BREAK

FWD
LEFT POD TOP VIEW
COOLING EXAUST 1

XMIT ANT
RCV ANT
FWD
PS 395
POD BREAK
PS 517
POD BREAK

RADOME
VIEW F
TAIL BREAK
FS 319
MODEM
RCV ANT
XMIT ANT
FS 608

The Precision Location Strike System (PLSS) was the most complicated payload carried by the U-2R at the time. It used a unique nose section and superpods, as well as filling the Q-bay with mission equipment. (U.S. Air Force)

Not heavily burdened with extra radomes and antennas, Article 051 (68-10329) approaches for a landing. Four-segment flaps make up most of the trailing edge of the wing. The flap segments were rearranged when the superpods were fielded, and even if the aircraft does not fly with superpods the flaps are not reconfigured. (Lockheed Martin Skunk Works via the Tony Landis Collection)

flight to a suspected ammunition storage area.

The deployment of the Son-of-Blade van allowed the SYERS to cover all of southern Iraq while remaining on-tether. By this time the U-2 could be dynamically retasked during flight. If a suspicious target was spotted, the U-2 could leave its planned track, examine the target, and relay the data back to Son-of-Blade. Photo interpreters would decide if the target warranted an immediate attack. If so, strike aircraft would hit the target and the U-2 would assess the damage. Also, when General Schwarzkopf wanted to assess the environmental damage from the Iraqis dumping oil into the Gulf, a SYERS-equipped U-2 diverted from its scheduled track to overfly the area.

Despite the invaluable real-time information ASARS-2 and SYERS were providing, in-theater commanders, especially Army commanders, wanted hard copy products. Although the systems could provide hard copy, the process required about 20 minutes and interfered with real-time collection. The U-2 began flying camera sorties to satisfy this need, but until the MIPE arrived in theater, film processing took several days. Before the aircraft had border-crossing authority, U-2s carried the Type-H camera and furnished spot imagery of targets inside Iraq. With border-crossing authority, the U-2 flew IRIS-III missions that covered more area, but with less clarity. Field commanders appreciated the additional coverage, but wanted greater resolution. The 1704th RS(P), decided to revise the Type-H camera mounting. Instead of looking at an angle, as it was designed to do, the camera would shoot

Article 060 (68-10338) was written-off at RAF Fairford on 29 August 1995. Its loss was particularly felt since the aircraft had been reconfigured to carry the SENIOR SPAN satellite system, and was routinely used for SENIOR GLASS missions. (Lockheed Martin Skunk Works via the Tony Landis Collection)

THROTTLE QUADRANT
(TR-1A/U-2R/ER-2)
(TR-1B Fwd Cockpit)

1 THROTTLE VERNIER
2 THROTTLE FRICTION
3 ROLL TRIM SWITCH
4 IDLE STOP
5 WING FLAP CONTROL
6 INTERMITTENT DUTY
   IGNITION SWITCH
7 MIC SWITCH
8 LIFT SPOILER SWITCH
9 SPEED BRAKE SWITCH

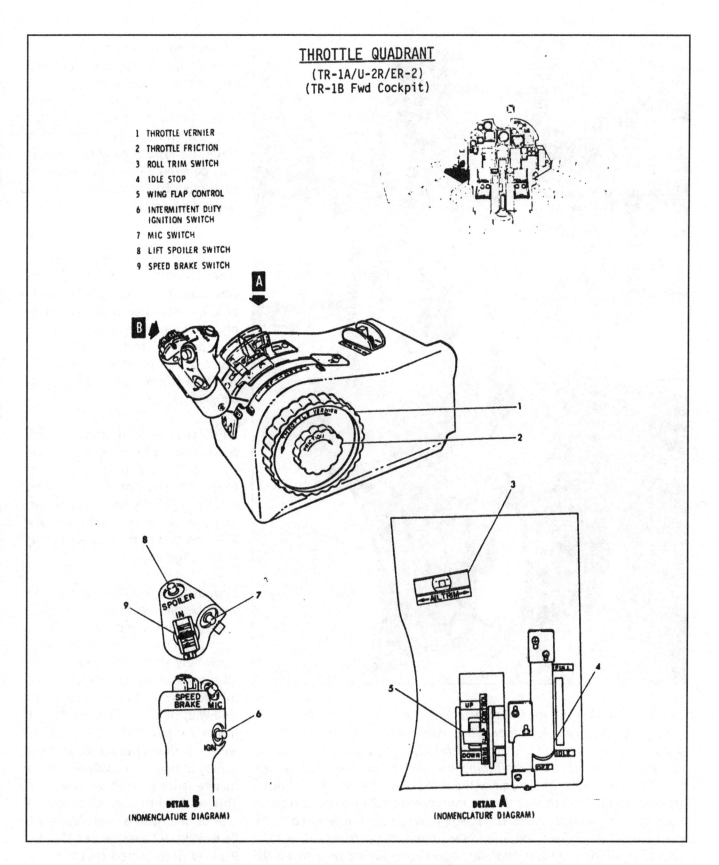

DETAIL **B**
(NOMENCLATURE DIAGRAM)

DETAIL **A**
(NOMENCLATURE DIAGRAM)

As throttles go in the modern world, this is a very simple one. Without having to worry about operating weapons systems and radar, the throttle quadrant is void of all the switches that complicate a modern jet fighter. In addition to the throttle itself, there are only six switches for the pilot to control: roll trim, wing flaps, lift spoilers, speed brakes, and microphone enable. (U.S. Air Force)

The U-2's rear tires are solid, not pneumatic like most aircraft tires. In the 1970s more durable polyurethane tires replaced the original rubber tires and worked well until 1990 when the tread began separating from the tire carcass. At Taif, where the aircraft sometimes had to taxi for a long distance, the U-2 would arrive at the end of the runway, ready for takeoff, with a separated rear tire. Although the tire manufacturer denied any change in the manufacturing process, the problem was eventually discovered. Environmental concerns had caused the manufacturer to replace aerosol cans of 5% silicon, used as a separating agent in the tire molds, with a 100% silicon solution applied with a cloth. The higher concentration of silicon prevented the polyurethane from adhering properly. Switching from silicon to Teflon solved the problem. (Lockheed Martin Skunk Works via the Tony Landis Collection)

straight down from nadir. Technicians at Taif had to remount and adjust the cameras, and mission planners had to develop new tracks, similar to the IRIS-III tracks, but less than three miles apart since the Type-H camera at nadir only covered a two-mile swath on each pass. The result was pictures beyond expectations.

A constant concern was the amount of JP-TS fuel on hand. When DESERT STORM began there was almost 450,000 gallons available, an estimated four week supply at five missions per day. When the operations tempo increased to seven sorties per day, the monthly JP-TS requirement increased to 600,000 gallons.

Ships and C-130 "bladder birds" brought in as much fuel as possible, but by the middle of February their was down only a two week supply. Luckily, it was a short war, and the decreased flight activity after the end of the war eased the shortage greatly.

Squadron activity peaked in the week before the 24 February 1991 onset of the ground war when the 1704 RS(P) had 12 aircraft and regularly flew seven sorties per day. In all, a total of 564 OLYMPIC FLARE missions were flown during the Gulf War, for a total of 4,561.6 flight hours. An additional 37 missions were scheduled but not flown for a variety of reasons, usually related to maintenance problems or weather. This equated to a mission capable rate of nearly 94%, well above the fleet-wide U-2 average of 83%. The 9th RW determined that the U-2 provided 30% of total intelligence, 50% of imagery intelligence, and 90% of all Army targeting intelligence during the Gulf War.

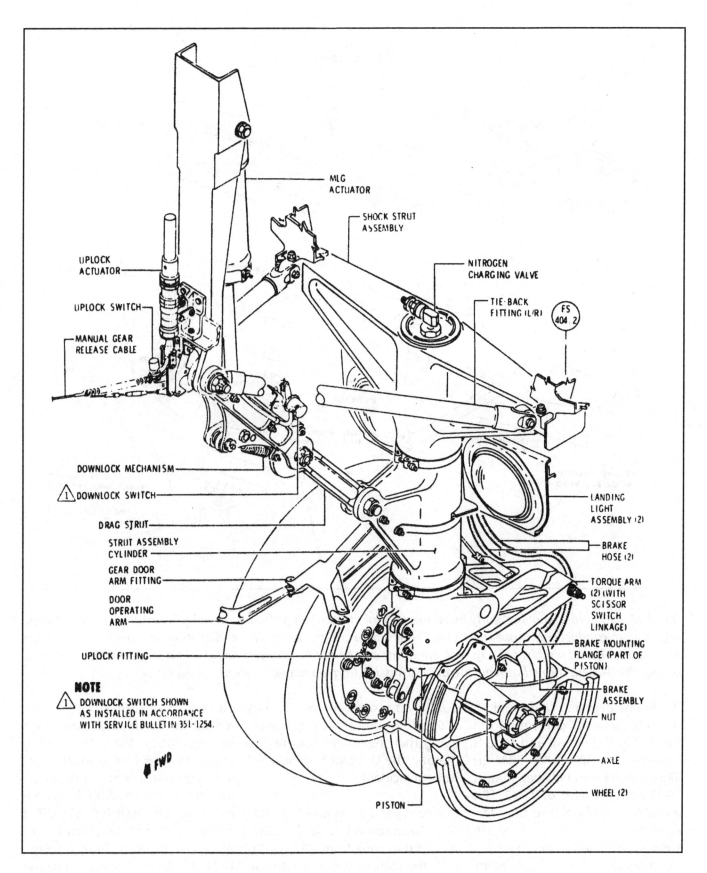

MLG ACTUATOR

SHOCK STRUT ASSEMBLY

UPLOCK ACTUATOR

UPLOCK SWITCH

MANUAL GEAR RELEASE CABLE

NITROGEN CHARGING VALVE

TIE-BACK FITTING (L/R)

FS 404.2

DOWNLOCK MECHANISM

⚠1 DOWNLOCK SWITCH

DRAG STRUT

STRUT ASSEMBLY CYLINDER

GEAR DOOR ARM FITTING

DOOR OPERATING ARM

UPLOCK FITTING

LANDING LIGHT ASSEMBLY (2)

BRAKE HOSE (2)

TORQUE ARM (2) (WITH SCISSOR SWITCH LINKAGE)

BRAKE MOUNTING FLANGE (PART OF PISTON)

BRAKE ASSEMBLY

NUT

AXLE

WHEEL (2)

PISTON

NOTE
⚠1 DOWNLOCK SWITCH SHOWN AS INSTALLED IN ACCORDANCE WITH SERVICE BULLETIN 351-1254.

◀ FWD

The main landing gear is located at the front of the U-2, and consists of two pneumatic tires on a single strut. Two landing lights are mounted on the forward edge of the strut. The strut does not swivel or turn, except on the U-2G aircraft modified for carrier duties. All braking forces are supplied by twin brakes on the main gear. (U.S. Air Force)

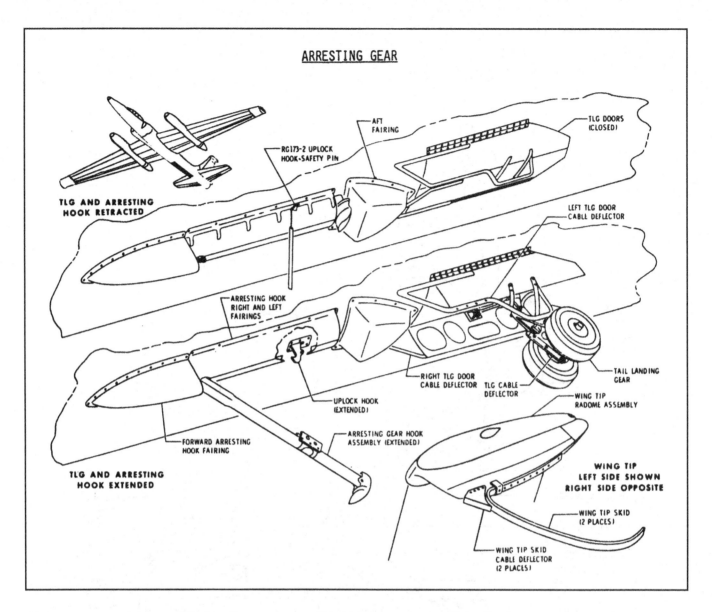

ARRESTING GEAR

The U-2R was carrier qualified early in its operational life, and all airframes were built with the reinforcements necessary to conduct carrier operations. Lockheed built a limited number of modification kits consisting of the tail hook assembly and various cable guards. These kits can be used to convert any U-2R on short notice. As far as is known, the U-2R has never flown an operational mission from an aircraft carrier. (U.S. Air Force)

U-2 flights over Iraq under United Nations auspices continue from Taif. Using the IRIS-III and Type-H cameras, over 300 OLIVE BRANCH flights were flown between August 1991 and the end of 1995. The Iraqis do not like it, and their foreign minister complained in March 1996 about the "… material and psychological damage caused by the violations of its airspace by this aircraft." The flights continued, regardless. In late 1997 the Iraqis publicly announced they would shoot down any U-2 caught overflying their territory. Despite the rhetoric, the U-2 flights continued without incident.

In recent years most attention has been focused on Bosnia. On ninehour round trips from RAF Alconbury, the 95th RS and its successor, OL-UK, used aircraft configured for either ASARS-2, SENIOR SPAN, or camera missions. When Alconbury closed, the three aircraft were moved temporarily to Fairford, then in December 1995 they were moved to Istres, France, which offers a shorter transit time to Bosnia. A new trailer-based SATCOM system codenamed MOBILE STRETCH located at Rimini, Italy, compresses ASARS-2 data downlinked from the U-2s. It is then transmitted to the lower-bandwidth DSCS satellites and transferred to Beale AFB, then on to UN forces.

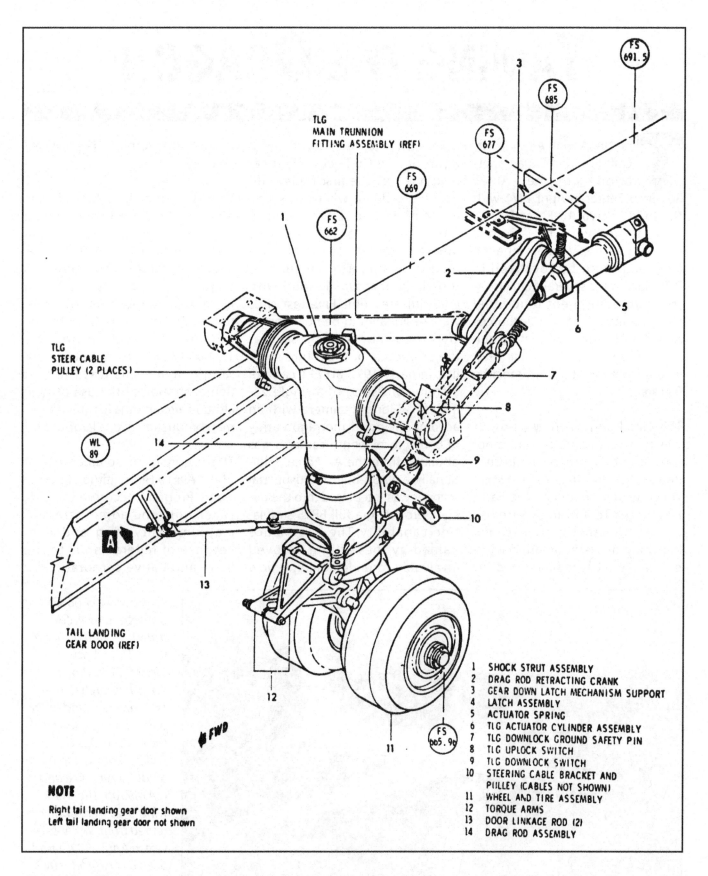

TLG
MAIN TRUNNION
FITTING ASSEMBLY (REF)

TLG
STEER CABLE
PULLEY (2 PLACES)

TAIL LANDING
GEAR DOOR (REF)

FWD

NOTE

Right tail landing gear door shown
Left tail landing gear door not shown

1 SHOCK STRUT ASSEMBLY
2 DRAG ROD RETRACTING CRANK
3 GEAR DOWN LATCH MECHANISM SUPPORT
4 LATCH ASSEMBLY
5 ACTUATOR SPRING
6 TLG ACTUATOR CYLINDER ASSEMBLY
7 TLG DOWNLOCK GROUND SAFETY PIN
8 TLG UPLOCK SWITCH
9 TLG DOWNLOCK SWITCH
10 STEERING CABLE BRACKET AND
   PULLEY (CABLES NOT SHOWN)
11 WHEEL AND TIRE ASSEMBLY
12 TORQUE ARMS
13 DOOR LINKAGE ROD (2)
14 DRAG ROD ASSEMBLY

Ground handling is accomplished by steering the rear wheels, much like a conventional tail-dragger. The rear tires are not pneumatic, and represent what are probably the last non-pneumatic aircraft tires in operational service. (U.S. Air Force)

TAMING THE DRAGON

The NASA High Altitude Aircraft Program began operation at the Ames Research Center in April 1971 with the loan of two Air Force U-2Cs. Prior to delivery the aircraft received extensive maintenance and repainting by Lockheed in Palmdale. After several familiarization and equipment functional check flights, the Earth Resources Aircraft Program began data acquisition flights on 31 August 1971 with a flight over the San Francisco Bay area.

The initial purpose of the project was to acquire multispectral photography to simulate the Return Beam Vidicon (RBV) data system which would be aboard the Earth Resources Technology Satellite (ERTS; LANDSAT). Four 70mm framing cameras were mounted vertically in the Q-bay to simultaneously image the same ground area. Equipped with 1.75-inch focal length lenses, the first three cameras were flown with black and white film, spectrally filtered to image the green, red, and near infrared portions of the electromagnetic spectrum, while the fourth camera was loaded with color infrared film. Five test sites were designated to be flown on an 18-day repetitive basis, the same as the orbit cycle of the future satellite. In early 1972 an A-1 camera system consisting of a single 24-inch focal length camera with an accompanying tri-metragon array of 6-inch focal length cameras was obtained from the Air Force. Additionally, a NASA-built multispectral scanner was integrated into the aircraft, providing a full ERTS simulation capability. The experience gained by these flights proved invaluable to understanding how to use and interpret the LANDSAT imagery.

The summer of 1972 brought the Arizona Land Use Experiment, a cooperative program between the state of Arizona, the U.S. Geological Survey, and NASA. This program acquired cloud-free black and white panchromatic metric photography that was utilized by the Geological Survey to produce 1:24,000-scale orthophoto quadrangle maps. This was the first demonstration of the use of high altitude aircraft data for quadrangle map production over a large area.

The inception and commencement of the Alaska High Altitude Photography Program occurred in 1978. Faced with the administration, mapping, surveying and conveyance of federal lands to the State and native corporations, a

Article 349 (65-6682) was transferred to NASA in June 1971 and assigned to the High Altitude Air Aircraft Program at Ames Research Center. The blue/grey and white paint scheme used by the NASA U-2Cs was a striking contrast to the all-black Air Force and CIA aircraft. The small wing U-2s were finally retired from NASA service in April 1989. It had been a very productive 17 years. (Lockheed Martin Skunk Works via Denny Lombard)

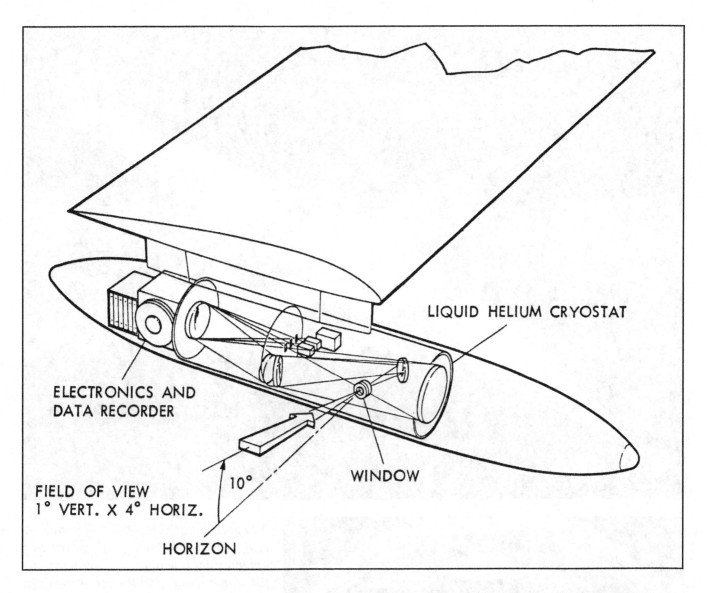

LIQUID HELIUM CRYOSTAT

ELECTRONICS AND
DATA RECORDER

FIELD OF VIEW
1° VERT. X 4° HORIZ.

10°

WINDOW

HORIZON

The Infrared Spectrometer (FLO) is a wing-mounted infrared spectral radiometer designed to investigate minor atmospheric constituents and their concentrations in the atmosphere. The radiometer was developed and operated by the University of Denver and looks out of the right wing pod at an angle of 10° above the horizon. Molecular radiation from the atmosphere enters through a zinc selenide window and is scanned by a liquid helium-cooled grating spectrometer. Up to 5.5 hours of data can be recorded on tape inside the pod. (NASA)

The ER-2s were transferred from the Ames Research Center to the Dryden Flight Research Center. The first (Article 063, N706NA) arrived at Dryden on 3 November 1997. By this time the aircraft had received the new NASA logo on its vertical stabilizer, replacing the NASA "worm" logo that had been carried for years. (NASA/DFRC via Tony Landis)

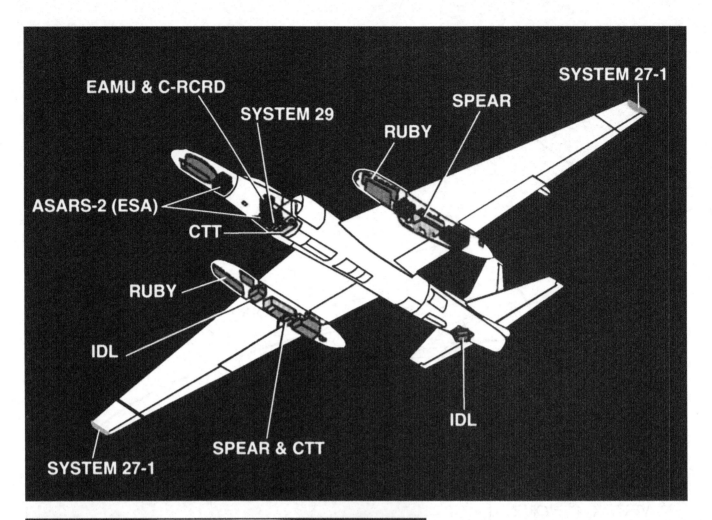

EAMU & C-RCRD

SYSTEM 29

SYSTEM 27-1

SPEAR

RUBY

ASARS-2 (ESA)

CTT

RUBY

IDL

IDL

SYSTEM 27-1

SPEAR & CTT

A fully-configured U-2R. The System 27-1 call-outs on the wing tips point out antennas for one of the ECM systems. The IDL references are to the real-time data link that allows the U-2 to transmit data directly to ground stations. (Lockheed Martin Skunk Works)

The cockpit on NASA's U-2Cs was generally similar to the operational aircraft flown by the Air Force and CIA. Obviously, the defensive electronics controls were missing, replaced by a variety of controls for the different research payloads. The U-2 used a control wheel instead of the stick used in most high performance aircraft since it was felt the wheel was easier to manipulate while wearing the pressure suit gloves on long flights. The driftsight dominates the forward instrument panel. Noteworthy are the two pencils in their holders on the control wheel. (Dennis R. Jenkins via the Mick Roth Collection)

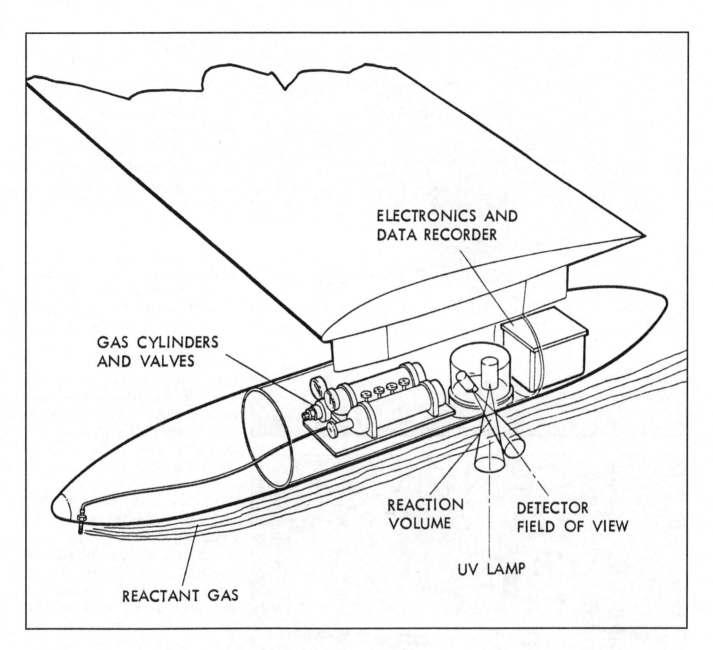

GAS CYLINDERS
AND VALVES

ELECTRONICS AND
DATA RECORDER

REACTANT GAS

REACTION
VOLUME

UV LAMP

DETECTOR
FIELD OF VIEW

The Resonance Fluorescence Experiment (REFLEX) system was designed to measure data on chlorine molecules in the stratosphere. This data relates to the hypothesis that the release of fluorochlorocarbons into the stratosphere may result in the catalytic decomposition of the Earth's ozone layer. The instrument includes two small sensors mounted inside a pod under the U-2's wing consisting of a special (resonance) ultraviolet (UV) light source and a photomultiplier, both of which are fitted with flowing oxygen filters. Each sensor is positioned to view a 60° cone downward into the stratosphere through a closed window in the pod. A nitric oxide (NO) ejector is positioned in the nose of the pod to release NO into the air stream. The NO reacts with chloride molecules in the stratosphere to produce chlorine which reflects the UV light and is detected by the photomultiplier. (NASA)

consortium of Federal and State agencies requested NASA's assistance in acquiring high altitude black and white and color infrared photography of the entire state. Over the next eight years, flights were conducted resulting in 95% of Alaska photographed with color infrared and black and white films with less than 10% cloud cover.

When the Air Force decided to reopen the U-2R production line, NASA was quick to order two of the new aircraft to replace their WB-57Fs and U-2Cs which were getting old and hard to maintain. The first ER-2 (Article 063; N706NA) made its initial flight on 11 May 1981 with Lockheed test pilot Art Peterson at the controls. The ER-2s delivered to

Article 063 (80-1063, N706NA) was the first of the last batch of U-2s to fly. NASA ordered two ER-2s along with the Air Force order for TR-1s. As it happened, the first aircraft off the line was a NASA ER-2. The "ER" stands for "Earth Resources" – the original U-2Cs had never officially been designated ER-1, but their legacy lived on. (NASA/DFRC via Tony Landis)

the NASA are capable of accommodating all of the existing U-2 sensor systems. Maximum payload weight is 3,750 pounds. Carrying a standard mission sensor complement, the aircraft has a normal endurance of 6.5 hours and a maximum altitude of approximately 75,000 feet A second purpose-built ER-2 (Article 097; N709NA) was delivered in 1989, by which time NASA had also "leased" an Air Force TR-1A (Article 069) as N708NA.

The story of the "leased" TR-1 began in October 1982 when a bus containing Air Force 17th RW security police was accidentally driven into a TR-1A (Article 069) at RAF Alconbury. The aircraft was repaired and subsequently redelivered to the 17th RW, but the pilots and ground crews insisted that it did not fly correctly, and the aircraft was retired to Lockheed's Palmdale facility. A decision was made to allow NASA to use the aircraft. All NASA U-2 maintenance is contracted to Lockheed, who promptly re-rigged the aircraft's control surfaces, and NASA pilots flew it for years without complaint.

The ER-2s were re-engined at the same time as the rest of the U-2R fleet, although their designation did not change. They also received most of the wiring upgrades that allow them to carry any of the sensors in the Air Force inventory, including the SENIOR SPAN satellite system. NASA is heavily dependent upon "hand-me-downs" from the Air Force for their sensors and other systems, although they obviously have little use for some of the more esoteric intelligence gathering systems. (NASA/DFRC via Tony Landis)

The first deployment of the ER-2 outside North America occurred in 1985 when one flew to England for a remote sensing campaign. This was followed in early 1987 with a deployment to Darwin, Australia, for

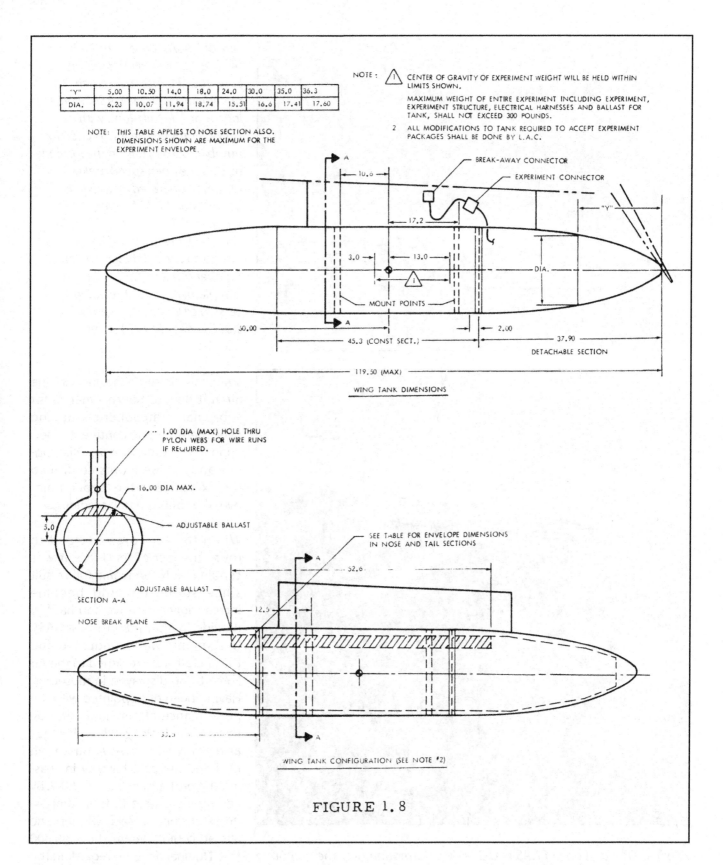

"Y"	5.00	10.50	14.0	18.0	24.0	30.0	35.0	36.3
DIA.	6.20	10.07	11.94	18.74	15.51	16.6	17.41	17.60

NOTE: THIS TABLE APPLIES TO NOSE SECTION ALSO. DIMENSIONS SHOWN ARE MAXIMUM FOR THE EXPERIMENT ENVELOPE.

NOTE: △ CENTER OF GRAVITY OF EXPERIMENT WEIGHT WILL BE HELD WITHIN LIMITS SHOWN.

MAXIMUM WEIGHT OF ENTIRE EXPERIMENT INCLUDING EXPERIMENT, EXPERIMENT STRUCTURE, ELECTRICAL HARNESSES AND BALLAST FOR TANK, SHALL NOT EXCEED 300 POUNDS.

2 ALL MODIFICATIONS TO TANK REQUIRED TO ACCEPT EXPERIMENT PACKAGES SHALL BE DONE BY L.A.C.

WING TANK DIMENSIONS

WING TANK CONFIGURATION (SEE NOTE #2)

FIGURE 1.8

When an experiment was loaded into one of the U-2C's underwing tanks, the opposite tank had to carry an equal amount of ballast. The tanks could be jettisoned by the pilot if required during an emergency. Like the CIA and Air Force U-2s, fuel could also be carried in the underwing tanks. When the underwing tanks were installed, the wing slipper tanks could not be carried due to weight and structural limitations. (NASA)

One of NASA's small wing U-2Cs (Article 349, N709NA) lands at Edwards AFB after a research mission in 1989. The NASA "worm" logo is on the tail along with its NASA number. The Air Force serial number (65-6682) is on the fuselage behind the open speed brake. Although operated by a civilian agency, most NASA aircraft still retain their military serial numbers since they are "on loan". NASA U-2s have also carried their complete "N" numbers on the rear fuselage to complement the abbreviated version carried on the vertical stabilizers. (NASA/DFRC via Tony Landis)

stratospheric sampling. In 1987 the aircraft flew to South America for sub-polar stratospheric sampling over the Antarctic continent, operating from Punta Arenas, Chile. Significantly, these flights confirmed the existence of the "ozone hole" over the southern polar region.

When the Air Force decided to retire the last of its U-2Cs, it was certain that NASA would follow suit since support would become increasingly expensive and hard to provide. In April 1989, the last NASA U-2C flights were conducted and the aircraft were returned to the Air Force to be displayed in museums. Having been disappointed with the performance of new high-altitude research vehicles such as Perseus and Strato-2C, NASA has even explored the possibility of increasing the performance of the ER-2. By adding removable 10-foot composite extensions to each wingtip, the aircraft could operate above 80,000 feet. No final decision regarding the modifications has been made, and it is unlikely that NASA would risk such valuable assets without a great deal of study.

The first ER-2 and one of NASA's U-2Cs fly in formation over the California coast. There are proposals to extend the wingtips of the ER-2 to enable them to achieve higher altitudes, something particularly practical now that they have received F118 engines. Funding constraints are likely to prohibit this for the foreseeable future however. (Lockheed Martin)

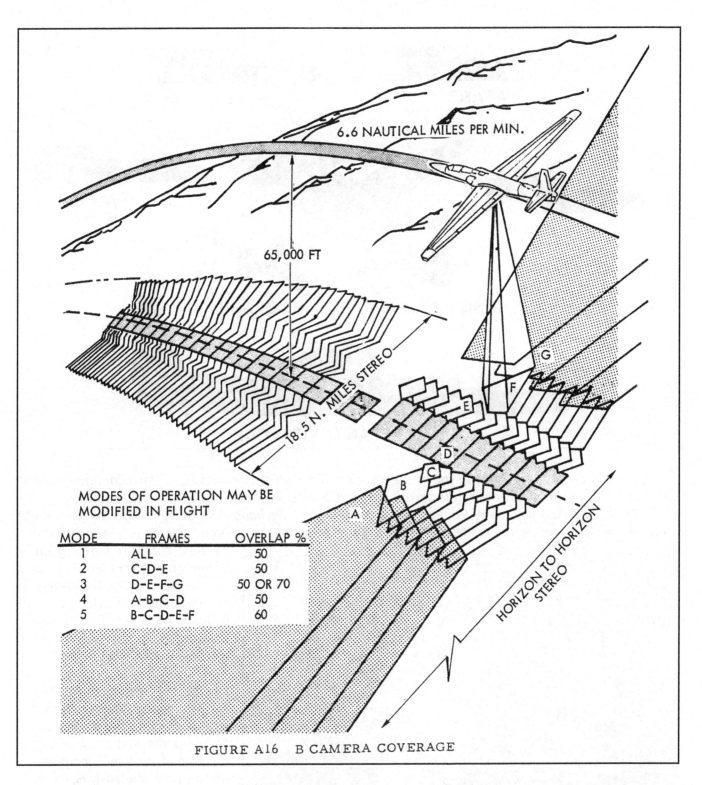

6.6 NAUTICAL MILES PER MIN.

65,000 FT

18.5 N. MILES STEREO

HORIZON TO HORIZON STEREO

G
F
E
D
C
B
A

MODES OF OPERATION MAY BE MODIFIED IN FLIGHT

MODE	FRAMES	OVERLAP %
1	ALL	50
2	C-D-E	50
3	D-E-F-G	50 OR 70
4	A-B-C-D	50
5	B-C-D-E-F	60

FIGURE A16   B CAMERA COVERAGE

The Type-B camera was the primary sensor used on reconnaissance overflights of denied territory. It has also been used by NASA to map various regions around the world. Type-B is a high-resolution camera with an HR-73B1 36-inch focal length f/10 lens designed to provide large-scale photography of large areas. The camera images on two 9.5-inch wide frames of film through a single lens, producing an 18x18-inch exposure. To provide horizon-to-horizon coverage, the lens indexes through seven positions: nadir; three left oblique; and three right oblique. Various combinations of these positions can be selected during operations. Camera operation is mechanically programmed to provide 50-70% overlap. The camera is fitted to an F210 Q-bay hatch. From an altitude of 65,000 feet, the Type-B camera can resolve objects on the ground as small as 12 inches. (NASA)

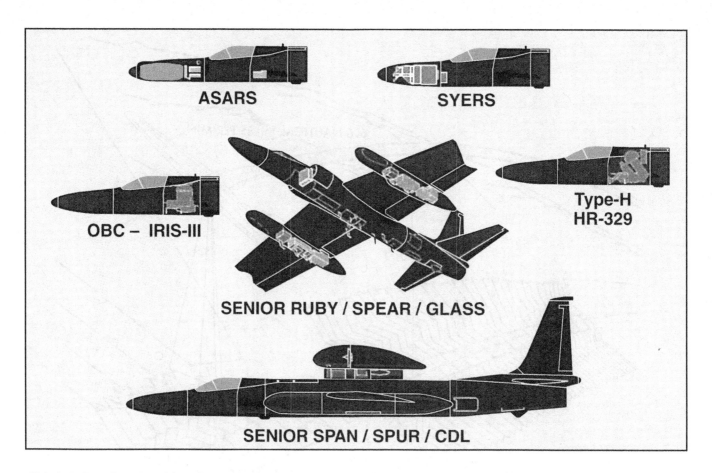

ASARS

SYERS

OBC – IRIS-III

Type-H
HR-329

SENIOR RUBY / SPEAR / GLASS

SENIOR SPAN / SPUR / CDL

This briefing from Lockheed Martin shows the location of the most common equipment configurations. A conscious attempt was made to separate aircraft systems from the payloads. Originally the U-2 concept was that any aircraft could carry any sensor (camera) through a series of interchangeable Q-bay hatches. As systems got more complex, and required more extensive wiring, this concept fell by the wayside. Certain aircraft were dedicated to particular sensors, greatly complicating scheduling and operational use. The U-2S program is attempting to provide sufficient wiring in each aircraft to allow any aircraft to carry any sensor. (Lockheed Martin Skunk Works)

Like the Air Force aircraft, NASA's ER-2 was generally seen without the superpods for the first few years. Later, experiments were devised that made good use of the superpods and the ER-2s started flying more regularly with them, particularly the "loaned" TR-1 which was configured for superpods from the beginning. The ER-2 also flies with experiments contained in pods hung under the wings, using the support structure installed for the superpods. (NASA/DFRC via Tony Landis)

WARBIRD**TECH**
SERIES

CODE NAMES

Angel	LADC	Lockheed Internal Name for U-2	1954
Aquatone	CIA	Aerial Reconnaissance Program (U-2)	1954
Automat	CIA	Photo intelligence Location in Washington D.C.	1956
Bald Eagle	USAF	Bell (Model 67/X-16), Martin (RB-57D), Fairchild Competition	1953
Beacon Hill	USAF	Aerial Reconnaissance Study Group	1951
Birdwatcher	LADC	Aircraft Performance Monitor	1960
Black Velvet	LADC	Very Flat Black Paint for U-2C	1965
Compass Arrow	USAF	Ryan Remotely Piloted Vehicle	1969
Camel Hump	USAF	U-2 operations from Taif, Saudi Arabia	1992
Chameleon	CIA	Cream-colored Paint for U-2C	1965
Cloudcraft	NAS	National Academy of Sciences Research Project	1966
Combat Dawn	USAF	Ryan Drone COMINT Operations	1970
Compass Cope	USAF	Boeing Remotely Piloted Vehicle	1973
Dirty Birds	LADC	U-2As covered in Radar Absorbing Material	1956
Genetrix	CIA/USAF	Spy Balloon project	1950-1957
Giant Dragon	USAF	Continued USAF U-2 Deployment to Vietnam	1968
Have Charity	USAF	Ballistic Missile Tracking Experiments	1967
Have Echo	USAF	Ballistic Missile Tracking Experiments	1967
Have Echo II	USAF	Ballistic Missile Tracking Experiments	1967
Hi Camp	USAF/NASA	Highly-Calibrated Airborne Measurements Program for Teal Ruby	1985
HiCAT	USAF	High Altitude Clear Air Turbulence Study	1964
Idealist	CIA	Alternate Name for AQUATONE	1954
Lariat	USAF	Ballistic Missile Tracking Experiments	1967
Lightning Bug	USAF	Ryan Firebee Reconnaissance Drones	1963
Lucky Dragon	USAF	USAF U-2 Deployment to Vietnam	1963
MIDAS	USAF	Missile Defense Alram System (Atlas-boosted)	1958
Moby Dick	USAF	Meteorological Balloons Used as Cover for Genetrix	1956
Muscle Magic	USAF	U-2 Missions Using Aerial Refueling	1963
Olympic Fire	USAF	Missions from Patrick AFB, Florida	1976
Olympic Harvest	USAF	Missions from RAF Akrotiri, Cyprus	1976
Olympic Torch	USAF	Missions from Osan AB, South Korea	1976
Operation Crowflight	USAF	High Altitude Sampling Program for U-2A	1956
Operation Overflight	CIA	Soviet Overflights	1957
Oscar Sierra	CIA	SA-2 SAM Missile Warning Receiver	1965
Overflight	CIA	Overflight Operations of 'Denied' Territory	1960
Pave Nickel	USAF	Target Location System for U-2C	
Pave Onyx	USAF	AN/ALQ-125 TEREC Target Location System for U-2C	
Program 461	USAF	Ballistic Missile Tracking Experiments	1966
Program 949	USAF	Continuation of Ballistic Missile Tracking Experiments	1967
Project 4076	USAF	Infra-Red Ballistic Missile Tracker	1967
Project TRIM	USAF	Target Radiation Intensity Measurement of Re-Entry Vehicles	1967
Purple Flash	CIA	Nuclear Seismic Sensor System	1958
Senior Blade	USAF	ELINT/SIGINT	
Senior Book	USAF	U-2 Vietnam SIGINT Operations	1968
Senior Jump	USAF	ELINT/SIGINT	

Senior Lance	USAF	Goodyear Synthetic Aperture Radar for U-2R	1973
Senior Open	USAF	LOROP Camera Nose System for U-2R	
Senior Ruby	USAF	E-Systems COMINT Collection System For U-2R	1977
Senior Saber	USAF	ELINT/SIGINT	
Senior Scout	USAF	ELINT/SIGINT	
Senior Shuffle	USAF	ELINT/SIGINT	
Senior Smart	USAF	ELINT/SIGINT	
Senior Span	USAF	U-2R 'C-Span III' with Satellite Data Link	
Senior Spear	USAF	Melpar COMINT Sensor for U-2R	1971
Senior Spur	USAF	ELINT/SIGINT	
Senior Stretch	USAF	ELINT/SIGINT in Superpods	
Senior Year	USAF	Project Office for SENIOR programs	
Smoky Joe	USAF	Two-Seat U-2Ds for Special Projects at Edwards	1960
SYERS	USAF	Senior Year Electro-Optic Relay System	
System 3	CIA	VHF COMINT	
System 4	CIA	TELINT system	
System 6	CIA	Wide Frequency Range ELINT (C-, L-, and X-Band)	
System 9	CIA	Granger airborne lock-breaker	1960
System 9B	CIA	Airborne Intercept Jammer	1962
System 12	CIA	SA-2 Fan Son Radar Warning Receiver	1962
System 13	CIA	Active ECM (Jammer)	1962
System 20	USAF	Airborne Intercept Jammer (Replaced System 9B)	1981
System 27	USAF	Radar Warning Receiver (Replaced System 12B)	1981
System 28	USAF	Active ECM (Jammer) (Replaced System 13)	1981
System 29	USAF	Missile Warning Receiver (Replaced Oscar Sierra)	1981
Teal Cameo	DARPA	Unmanned TR-1 Replacement (not proceeded with)	
Tell Two	USAF	SIGINT B-47 variants	1960
The Ranch	CIA	Groom Lake Flight Test Facility	1956
Trojan Horse	USAF	Continued USAF U-2 Deployment to Vietnam	1966
Watertown Strip	CIA	Groom Lake Flight Test Facility	1956

U-2 Variants

U-2A	Basic small wing U-2 with J57 engine
U-2B	Proposed bomber variant.
U-2C	U-2As with J75 engines and larger intakes
U-2C(T)	U-2C Trainer
U-2D	Two-place aircraft (2 aircraft)
U-2E	U-2A with in-flight refueling (3 aircraft)
U-2F	U-2C with in-flight refueling (5 aircraft)
U-2G	U-2C with carrier equipment (3 aircraft)
U-2H	U-2F with carrier equipment (1 aircraft)
U-2R	Basic big wing U-2 with J75 engine
U-2R(T)	U-2R Trainer
U-2S	U-2R with F118 engine
U-2S(T)	U-2R(T) with F118 engine
TR-1A	Same as U-2R
TR-1B	Same as U-2R(T)
ER-2	U-2R for NASA

AB	Air Base
ACC	Air Combat Command
AFB	Air Force Base
ALSS	Advanced Location Strike System
AM	Amplitude Modulation
ASARS	Advanced Synthetic Aperture Radar System
CIA	Central Intelligence Agency
COMINT	Communications Intelligence
CRAF	Civil Reserve Air Fleet
CW	Continuous Wave
ECM	Electronic Counter Measures
ELINT	Electronics Intelligence
EP-X	Electronics Patrol - Experimental
FM	Frequency Modulation
GE	General Electric
GPS	Global Positioning System
HASP	High Altitude Sampling Program
HiCAT	Hi-altitude Clear Air Turbulence program
IRBM	Intermediate Range Ballistic Missile
IRIS	Intelligence Reconnaissance Imaging System
IRS	Internal Revenue Service
JP-TS	Low Vapor Pressure Fuel
LF-1A	Low Vapor Pressure Fuel
LOROP	Long-Range Oblique Photographic (camera)
MIPE	Mobile Intelligence Processing Element
MTI	Moving Target Indicator
NACA	National Advisory Committee for Aeronautics
NASA	National Aeronautics and Space Administration
OL	Operating Location
P&W	Pratt & Whitney
PLSS	Precision Location Strike System
RAF	Royal Air Force
RBV	Return Beam Vidicon
RoCAF	Republic of China Air Force
RPV	Remotely Piloted Vehicle
RS(P)	Reconnaissance Squadron (Provisional)
RW	Reconnaissance Wing
SAC	Strategic Air Command
SIGINT	Signals Intelligence
SLATS	Signal Location and Targeting System
SRS	Strategic Reconnaissance Squadron
SRW	Strategic Reconnaissance Wing
SSB	Single Side Band
SYERS	SENIOR YEAR Electro-optical Reconnaissance System
TAC	Tactical Air Command
TRAC	Tactical Radar Correlator
TREDS	TR-1 Exploitation Demonstration System
TRIGS	TR-1 Ground Station
UAV	Unmanned Aerial Vehicle
WBFM	Wide Band Frequency Modulation
WRSP	Weather Reconnaissance Squadron, Provisional

SIGNIFICANT DATES

MAY 1951
BEACON HILL study group meets to discuss aerial reconnaissance systems

MARCH 1953
Specification for high altitude reconnaissance platform completed by U.S. Air Force

JULY 1953
BALD EAGLE contracts awarded to Bell, Fairchild, and Martin

18 MAY 1954
Unsolicited proposal for Lockheed Model CL-282 submitted to U.S. Air Force as BALD EAGLE contender

7 JUNE 1954
Kelly Johnson notified CL-282 proposal was rejected

19 NOVEMBER 1954
Johnson begins conversations with Central Intelligence Agency about modified CL-282

9 DECEMBER 1954
$54 million contract for 20 aircraft received from CIA

DECEMBER 1954
BEACON HILL group defines Type-B camera specifications

8 AUGUST 1955
Tony LeVier makes first "official" U-2 flight at Groom Lake

OCTOBER 1955
Bell X-16 (BALD EAGLE winner) is cancelled as redundant to U-2

18 OCTOBER 1955
U-2 achieves its design altitude of 73,000 feet

DECEMBER 1955
Lockheed receives go-ahead for 30 additional aircraft

EARLY 1956
First class of six CIA pilots arrive at Groom Lake

20 JUNE 1956
First operational U-2 mission flown by Carl Overstreet photographs Warsaw, the Prague, and portions of East Germany

4 JULY 1956
First overflight of the Soviet Union takes Harvey Stockman over Minsk and Leningrad

10 JULY 1956
Soviet Union lodges diplomatic complaint regarding U-2 overflights

JUNE 1957
U.S. Air Force begins to receive U-2 aircraft

1 MAY 1960
CIA pilot Francis Gary Powers is shot down over Sverdlovsk

OCTOBER 1962
U-2s detect Soviet missiles in Cuba, bringing the world to the brink of nuclear war

27 OCTOBER 1962
Major Rudolph Anderson's U-2 is shot down over Cuba. The next day the Soviets announce they will withdraw the missiles.

4 AUGUST 1963
Bob Schumacher carrier qualifies the U-2G

MAY 1964
PROJECT SEEKER uses a U-2G to monitor French nuclear tests from an aircraft carrier

SEPTEMBER 1966
12 revised U-2Rs ordered from Lockheed

28 AUGUST 1967
Bill Park takes the U-2R on its maiden flight from North Base at Edwards AFB

DECEMBER 1968
The last U-2R is delivered

EARLY 1973
Navy conducts test of EP-X concept using two borrowed CIA U-2Rs

AUGUST 1970
CIA U-2Rs begin flights over the Middle East from RAF Akrotiri, Cyprus

APRIL 1971
Two U-2Cs released to NASA for research flights

APRIL 1976
The last U-2 is finally withdrawn from Thailand

16 NOVEMBER 1979
After a 12 year lapse, production of new U-2Rs (and TR-1s) begins

11 MAY 1981
First ER-2 makes its maiden flight with Art Peterson at the controls

AUGUST 1981
ASARS-1 prototype begins flight tests on U-2R

1 AUGUST 1981
First TR-1 makes maiden flight with Ken Weir at the controls

JANUARY 1983
First two-seat TR-1B is delivered

12 FEBRUARY 1983
The first European-based TR-1 arrives at RAF Alconbury

APRIL 1989
Last NASA and Air Force U-2Cs retired

17 AUGUST 1990
Two U-2Rs arrive in Saudi Arabia as part of DESERT SHIELD, and fly first OLYMPIC FLARE mission two days later

OCTOBER 1991
All remaining TR-1s are redesignated U-2Rs

12 AUGUST 1994
First re-engined U-2S makes its maiden flight

CPSIA information can be obtained
at www.ICGtesting.com
Printed in the USA
LVOW03s0239281115

464480LV00025B/706/P